Collection of Sermons

"Helping You Reach Your Full Potential

In Messiah"

By

Joseph A. Chandler

ISBN 978-1-105-08386-0

© Copyright 2011 – 2013 Joseph Chandler

All rights reserved. This book is protected by the copyright laws of the United States of America. This book may not be copied or reprinted for commercial gain or profit. The use of short quotations or occasional page copying for personal or group study is permitted and encouraged. Permission will be granted upon request. Unless otherwise identified, Scriptures taken from the HOLY BIBLE, NEW INTERNATIONAL VERSION, Copyright © 1973, 1978, 1984 International Bible Society. Used by permission of Zondervan Bible Publishers.

Joseph Chandler
In Him Ministries
PO Box 449
Jackson, SC 29831

"Helping You Reach Your Full Potential In Messiah!"

2013 Edition

ISBN 978-1-105-08386-0

Photo: Rev. F. V. Chandler, Jr. taken in 1968

This first sermon is in loving memory of my father, Rev. Floyd Vernon Chandler, Jr. who went to be with the LORD on November 8, 1993.

This was typed from his notes of his last sermon given in Hendersonville, NC on October 17, 1993 while camping with the Travel Master Club.

I CAN SLEEP WHEN THE WIND BLOWS

By: Rev. Floyd Vernon Chandler, Jr.

Scripture: Ecclesiastes 1:1-11,

Text 1:6 "The wind blows to the south and turns to the north; round and round it goes."

(Ecclesiastes 1-11 NIV)

[1] The words of the Teacher, son of David, king in Jerusalem: [2] "Meaningless! Meaningless!" says the Teacher. "Utterly meaningless! Everything is meaningless." [3] What do people gain from all their labors at which they toil under the sun? [4] Generations come and generations go, but the earth remains forever.

⁵ The sun rises and the sun sets, and hurries back to where it rises. ⁶ The wind blows to the south and turns to the north; round and round it goes, ever returning on its course. ⁷ All streams flow into the sea, yet the sea is never full. To the place the streams come from, there they return again.

⁸ All things are wearisome, more than one can say. The eye never has enough of seeing, nor the ear its fill of hearing. ⁹ What has been will be again, what has been done will be done again; there is nothing new under the sun.

¹⁰ Is there anything of which one can say, "Look! This is something new"? It was here already, long ago; it was here before our time. ¹¹ No one remembers the former generations, and even those yet to come will not be remembered by those who follow them."

Key Text 1:6 "The wind blows …. round and round it goes."

A farmer was hiring a young farm hand. The farmer asked one young man what he could do. The boy gave a surprising answer: "I can sleep when the wind blows." The farmer wasn't sure what he meant by this, but he hired the boy.

Sometime later, a heavy wind and rain storm came up during the night. The farmer took his lantern and went out to the big barn to see if all was in order. He was pleased to find that everything was in good shape. The barn doors and shutters were closed tightly and barred. The cows were bedded down in clean straw. The straw pile had been secured with a canvas firmly tied down over the top. The windmill was shut off and lever down. It was then that the farmer knew what his young farmhand meant when he said that he could sleep when the wind blows.

Can we sleep when the wind blows? Did we close the windows? Did we put the awning up securely? Did we park away from trees with dead limbs? If electricity goes off, are the batteries on full power? Did we fix that leaky roof?

In life, **"The wind blows ... round and round it goes."** Nothing is ever exactly the same as the day before. Mothers and fathers, you have the same children you had yesterday.....but today will be different....they will find new ways to aggravate you.....and new ways to make you love them.

We hear the remarks: I've got to go back to the same old job, the same old school, the same old house...etc. Not so....you're not even the same old person from one day to the next. We are a day older. We have learned more or we have forgotten something. We are either better than yesterday or we are worse.

What will the whirling winds bring tomorrow? Will they bring storms or fair weather? Will they bring rain or sunshine? Will they bring sickness or health? How long will each last? Will tomorrow bring partial war over the world, an uneasy peace, total war, total destruction or a better understanding between people? We don't know.

(2 Peter 3:1-14 NIV) "Dear friends, this is now my second letter to you. I have written both of them as reminders to stimulate you to wholesome thinking. I want you to recall the words spoken in the past by the holy prophets and the command given by our Lord and Savior through your apostles."

"First of all, you must understand that in the last days scoffers will come, scoffing and following their own evil desires. They will say, "Where is this coming' he promised? Ever since our fathers died, everything goes on as it has since the beginning of creation." But they deliberately forget that long ago by God's word the heavens existed and the earth was formed out of water and by water. By these waters also the world of that time was deluged and destroyed. By the same world the present heavens and earth are reserved for

fire, being kept for the day of judgment and destruction of ungodly men."

"But do not forget this one thing, dear friends: With the Lord a day is like a thousand years, and a thousand years are like a day. The lord is not slow in keeping his promise, as some understand slowness. He is patient with you, not wanting anyone to perish, but everyone to come to repentance."

"But the day of the Lord will come like a thief. The heavens will disappear with a roar; the elements will be destroyed by fire, and the earth and everything in it will be laid bare."

"Since everything will be destroyed in this way, what kind of people ought you to be? You ought to live holy and godly lives as you look forward to the day of God and speed its coming. That day will bring about the destruction of the heavens by fire, and the elements will melt in the heat. But in keeping with his promise we are looking forward to a new heaven and a new earth, the home of righteousness."

"So then dear friends, since you are looking forward to this, make every effort to be found spotless, blameless and at peace with him." (2 Peter 3:1-14 NIV)

Can you sleep when the wind blows? When old age creeps up on you? When you or your loved ones become ill? When your friends forsake you? When you've spent all your money on doctors and medicines? When death knocks on your door?

As Job's would be friend - **"If you just had enough faith!"** I know God can heal, but people with all the faith in the world, get sick and die.

I accepted Jesus Christ when the wind was not blowing so severely - I didn't accept him so that I would never get old or sick - but for my Savior - to be with me in old age - sickness - even death. With Christ as our Savior, we can sleep in the middle of all storms. **"The wind blows ... round and round it goes."** Can you sleep when the when blows?

If you would like to sleep when the wind blows all around and around, then you too need to accept Jesus. Ask the Lord Jesus to come into your life and to be your Savior and Lord. Ask Him to forgive your sins, and to give you the gift of eternal life with Him today.

Picture of Rev. Joseph A. Chandler while the minister at Jackson Christian Fellowship Church as well as the Emergency Responder Chaplain at the Jackson Volunteer Fire Dept. in Jackson, SC. 1996 – 1998.

The remaining sermons I preached at one time or another at one church or service during the years. I don't take credit that they are totally original ideas or concepts from me. I have attempted to give credit as best I can. I came across all of these notes recently while going through some old saved computer disks. Many were typed up over ten years ago when I had preached them. This is not a complete record due to many of the notes of the messages have gone misplaced at this time. But what follows should record a baseline of the messages shared during the years. These can also be applied today to other churches as well as the whole Body of Messiah.

REMEMBER THE BASICS

Have you ever felt uncomfortable or even a little afraid to get up in front of people and give a talk, a Bible Study, or even to preach a message? I think this is normal for most of us. Yes there are a few that never get butterflies in their stomach when they get up before people to speak. But even those people at one time probably felt uncomfortable. The Bible tells us in **Romans 1:16 (NIV), "I am not ashamed of the gospel..."** Jesus told us to Go make disciples of all nations and that He will be with us always. **(Matt.28:20)** But even though this is true we sometimes let our fears hold us back.

Let me tell you a story to illustrate this. This story took place at a Christian Camp up in the mountains early in the month of June. This was the week of training for the Staff Members. This was the week before all of the other campers would start to arrive for their summer of adventure. It was during a week of training to see who would make it as a Counselor for the summer.

There was one person there, named John that was a quiet person. John loved the Lord but he did not feel comfortable getting up in front of a group and talking. John knew, however, that part of this week of training called for him to lead in some type of devotional. So at the beginning of the week John went to the Camp Director and explained his fear and asked the Director to please not ask him to lead in any of the services. John told the Director that he would gladly clean up the mess hall daily, cut the grass, pick up garbage, and even clean the latrines. Anything but speak before the other Staff Members.

The Camp Director listened very sympathetically to John and saw that John was really afraid to speak before a group. But the Director also knew that speaking before a group was the very thing that he needed to do. So the Director told John that tomorrow morning he would lead in the morning devotional and prayer before breakfast. John did not know what he was going to do. He read through the Bible trying to come up with something that he felt he could say, but nothing seemed to happen. John did not sleep much that night.

The next morning as the other Staff Members gathered for the devotional, John felt kind of sick. He still had nothing planned to speak on. John stepped up to the podium. You could almost see his knees shaking. He cleared his throat and looked around at the people gathered there. And then he asked a question. *"Does anybody here know what I am going to say?"* They all said, *"No."* John hesitated for a moment as the sweat started to bead up on his forehead. Then he said, *"I don't know either, so let's pray. God, thank you for this food and please watch over us today. Amen."*

Well the Director looked over at John with compassion and went over to him and said to John that he knew that he could do it and told him to try it again at lunch time. John went to breakfast but did not eat much that morning. He had to face the group again in just a few hours.

Lunch time came before John knew it. John knew that the other Staff Members had been talking about how he did the morning devotional. They just knew that John would not make it as a Camp Counselor. John stood up again holding on to the podium for his legs were weak. John looked around at all the people gathered there. John opened his mouth as to say something but nothing came out. John cleared his throat and tried again. This time he asked the same question as before. *"Do you know what I am going to say?"* The group knew that John didn't know either so they responded with a, *"Yes, we know."* John said, *"Well, if you know then I don't need to tell you, so let's pray. God, thank you for this food and continue to watch over us today. Amen."*

The Camp Director went to John again and told him that he knew that John could do it. The Camp Director told him that tonight would be his last chance. If he could not deliver a meaningful message this time he would not be able to be on staff.

John did not even go into the mess hall to eat lunch. He went to his cabin and closed his door and cried out to God. He prayed to God to help him. He studied the Bible. He told God that he could not do it. If it was to be done, it would be up to God. He continued to pray, read and surrender his life, body, soul, and mind to God. He asked God to turn this day around for His good. He asked God to give him the words and the courage to speak the message that the Holy Spirit wanted. He spent the whole afternoon there in his cabin before the Lord.

Supper time had come. The group was assembled waiting on John. John finally came up to the podium. He had no notes in his hands. The only thing in his hand was a Bible. Something was different though. He seemed to be at peace. Had he given up on being on staff? Would he deliver a message? John cleared his throat as he looked deep into the eyes of all present. Then he started off just as he had the last two times. Yet this time there was something different in his voice. He asked, *"Do you know what I am going to say?"*

The Camp Director looked at John and then toward the ground while shaking his head. The other staff members were mixed on how to respond. Some in the group responded with a *"YES"*. Others responded with a *"NO"*, for surely John had come up with something to say. John waited for what seemed like forever. He closed his eyes for a second as if to pray. The whole group was quiet and looking at John for his next response. John then opened his mouth and said, **"Those that know -- Go tell those that don't!"**

There is a message there. The message is very basic. Sometimes we overlook the Basics. We need to remember the Basics. After Jesus rose from the dead he gave us what is known as the Great Commission. **"...Jesus came to them and said, "All authority in heaven and on earth has been given to me. Therefore go and make disciples of all nations, baptizing them in the name of the Father and of the Son and of the Holy Spirit, and teaching them to obey everything I have commanded you. And surely I am with you always, to the very end of the age." Matthew 28:18-20 (NIV)**

GO - MAKE - DISCIPLES.

If we would just do this we could insure that the whole world would have a chance to say "YES" to Jesus in our lifetime. Let us look at the following example dealing with duplication of discipleship.

Let's take 20 people. Just a small amount when one looks at all that confesses Jesus as Lord and Savior. But let's say that these 20 people go out and find one person each that is willing to be a disciple. These 20 spend time helping these new disciples grow. The next year there would be 40 ready to go out to find one to disciple. Year 3 there would be 80, and so on. In just 12 years there would be 40,960 disciples. In 24 years there would be 167,772,160 disciples. All of these just from 20 committed people today willing to obey Jesus. If all Christians today would do the same the Gospel would be preached to every person in the world in our lifetime.

I think God is telling us to remember the Basics. What about you? Is God saying, "Those that Know - Go tell those that don't"? Are you in the group that knows or the group of the ones that don't? What group do you want to be in? And what are we going to do about it?

Today we all can make a choice that will change not only our lives, but will also change the whole world. Jesus died for you. Will you live for Him? Will we do the part God has called us to do? Will we carry out the Great Commission? Will we remember the Basics? ***"Those that know - Go tell those that don't!"***

ACCEPT AND BE THANKFUL FOR THE UNIVERSAL GIFTS OFFERED BY GOD

God is the giver of great gifts. God created this world and everything in it. That includes each one of us. We were created and designed for a reason. We were created in the image of God and we were created to commune with God. God is Love. He wants each of us to fulfill what we were designed for universally. God is continuing offer gifts to us today. Some of us accept them, some of us refuse them, but God still offers them to all people universally.

When a gift is given in love it should be important to both the giver and the receiver. Gifts of friendship, love, and compassion are just some of the kinds of gifts that we can offer and receive. Many times we may turn our backs on some of these gifts and not receive them. Sometimes we will take them for granted and just set them aside to rot. Yes, there are times when we have been given a gift that we fail to accept it and fail to say "Thank You".

Not only do people give gifts, as already mentioned, but God gives gifts also. He has given us this Earth to live on. On this Earth and in our solar system God has provided everything that is required for life. God has given us water. Our bodies require an intake of water on a regular basis in order to live. If we choose not to receive this water we would soon die. We often take water for granted. When was the last time we stopped and thanked God for the water?

God has given us the Sun. Scientists tell us that without the Sun all life on our planet would die. We need the Sun in order to live. Can we imagine constructing some type of a barrier around our world that would keep us from receiving the Sun's energy? To do this would be foolish because without the Sun there would be certain death. When was the last time we thanked God for giving us the Sun?

God has also given us His one and only Son. The Word of God tells us that without accepting this free gift offered to all that we will perish. It is truly the gift of Life. The gift of having God Live In Us. It is what we were designed for. It is offered to all universally. You cannot earn it. It is freely given. All we have to do is to accept it and tell God "Thank You". The Bible tells us in **2 Corinthians 5:19 (NIV),** *"that God was reconciling the world to himself in Christ, not counting men's sins against them."* The Good News that should be our Universal Herald is that God loves us so much that he has already forgiven everybody's sin. God is telling us that he has forgiven everybody's sins universally. This is truly Good News. We all need to take hold of this free gift and accept it.

God Has Already Forgiven All People. We Just Need To Accept His Free Universal Gift!

Sometimes our eyes need to be opened to see the truth clearer. The Bible says:

Romans 3:23 (NIV): *"For all have sinned and fall short of the glory of God."*

We need to see that we have all fallen short of being perfect.

Romans 6:23 (NIV): *"For the wages of sin is death, but the gift of God is eternal life in Christ Jesus our Lord."*

Romans 5:8 (NIV): *"But God demonstrates His own love for us in this: While we were yet sinners, Christ died for us."*

John 3:16 (NIV): *"For God so loved the world that He gave His one and only Son, that whoever believes in Him shall not perish but have eternal life."*

John 14:6 (NIV): (Jesus speaking), *"I am the way and the truth and the life. No one comes to the Father except through Me."*

God has forgiven us if we will accept it. Can we imagine constructing some type barrier to keep us from receiving this forgiveness? We may say, "But I don't believe a loving God would condemn us." Guest what? He doesn't.

John 3:17-18 (NIV): *"for God did not send his Son into the world to condemn the world, but to save the world through him. Whoever believes in him is not condemned, but whoever does not believe stands*

condemned already because he has not believed in the name of God's one and only Son."

Another way to say it might be that we are like a small child playing in the middle of a very busy super highway. If we stay in the highway playing we are condemned to be hurt or killed. But if we let our parents lead us safely away for the road unto a safe fenced in playground then we live. We have the choice. What would yours be?

One may say, "I believe in the religion of Jesus, not the religion about Jesus." When we really look at the recorded information of Jesus we can see clearer. Jesus did come out and say that he was God. After all, that is why the religious leaders had him killed. Can we say that he was a great teacher even if he lied about who he claimed to be? We need to look at his whole life, teachings and actions. We should not just pick out the parts that we want to in order to not deal with the truth. We really should look at his whole life, teachings and action to find the Truth. When we do this we can only come up with one of three conclusions. These same conclusions are found in Josh McDowell's book "More Than A Carpenter".

He was a Liar? If this is true then his lifestyle or religion is one of going around deceiving and lying. He said he was God. He said that he was the only way.

He was a Lunatic? Maybe he really thought that he was God, but was mistaken? After all, it is possible to be both sincere and wrong. But how can a lunatic go around doing good and healing all who were under the power of the devil? How can a lunatic die and the three days later rise from the dead?

He is Lord! He was and is who He said He was. If He is who He said He is, then one day every knee shall bow before Him and every tongue will confess that He is Lord. (see **Philippians 2:10-11**) The only question then is when will we confess the truth? Will we confess it now or later? Before we die or after?

What about you and me? Will we receive the free gift of forgiveness? Will we choose to believe in, trust in, Jesus and receive in Christ the forgiveness and the eternal life? Will we let our loving parent lead us from the danger of the super highway to the safety of the fenced in playground or will we stay where we are and remain condemned.

God as well as family and friends are always trying to give us many other gifts. The gifts might be a word of encouragement, some type of spiritual insight into choices we may need to make, or maybe something material. Are we refusing to receive them? Maybe it is time to get by ourselves and really think about all the gifts that are offered to us. Maybe it is time to really talk to God and accept his loving hand to lead us to his safety.

Let us start anew today and take time to really "receive" the gifts given in love and use them for what they are intended for. Let us share gifts with others. Let us remember to say "Thank You". You can accept God freely offered universal gift of eternal life with him today. He is waiting for you to reach up and accept His gift today. God is love. Will you accept His Love Today?

The Greatest Commandments

Now, we all remember some of the Ten Commandments that God gave us through Moses at Mt. Sinai. Let me review them here. These are in short form here as taken from the Kingdom Chums video called "Original Top Ten". See Exodus 20 for exact wording from the Bible.

1) Only One God.

2) No Idols.

3) No Swearing With God's Name.

4) Keep God's Day Special.

5) Honor Your Father and Mother.

6) Do Not Kill.

7) No Adultery, Be Loyal.

8) Don't Steal.

9) Don't Lie.

10) Don't Covet.

From that time, approximately 1300 BC, until the time of Jesus Christ, these were the guidelines to live by. What happened then when Jesus Christ came? Jesus said, *"Do not think that I have come to abolish the Law or the Prophets; I have not come to abolish them but to fulfill them."* **(Matt. 5:17 NIV)**

Jesus then goes on to explain some of these commandments in Matthew 5 starting with the 21st verse. *"You have heard that it was said to the people long ago, 'Do not murder, and anyone who murders will be subject to judgment.' But I tell you that anyone who is angry with his brother will be subject to judgment."* **(Matt. 5:21-22 NIV)**

Now let us go down to verse 27. *"You have heard that it was said, 'Do not commit adultery.' But I tell you that anyone who looks at a woman lustfully has already committed adultery with her in his heart."* **(Matt. 5:27-28 NIV)**

So we can see here that it is not only what we do physically, but it is also what we think. It is what is in our minds. You see, sin starts in our mind with what we think. The world today is full of things to introduce sin in our minds. But we as Christians need to recondition our minds to the way of our Lord. You see not only sin starts with a thought, but also Praise, Worship, Good Works and Deeds. They all start with a thought.

How do we recondition our mind to follow Jesus better? The following are just some suggestions:

1) Daily Reading from God's Word.

2) Daily Devotionals.

3) Daily Confessions of What God Says About Us.

4) Pray Daily. (Without Ceasing)

5) Go and Be Involved In Church.

6) Listen to Christian Radio, Christian Music, and Christian TV.

7) Do His Will, Follow Him, Do His Commands.

In Matthew 22, Jesus was asked about the commandments and which were the greatest. Jesus told them, **"Love your God with all your heart and with all your soul and with all your mind, This is the first and greatest commandment. And the second is like it, Love your neighbor as yourself. All the Law and**

*Prophets hang on these two commandments." * **(Matt. 22:37-40 NIV)**

LOVE GOD - - and - - LOVE YOUR NEIGHBOR

Let us look at these two commandments starting with loving your neighbor. We learn from the Bible that your neighbor is anyone that is not yourself. This includes your enemies. We see this in Luke chapter 6 starting with verse 27.

Jesus says, *"But I tell you who hear me: Love your enemies, do good to those who hate you, bless those who curse you, pray for those who mistreat you. If someone strikes you on one cheek, turn to him the other also. If someone takes your cloak, do not stop him from taking your tunic. Give to everyone who asks you, and if anyone takes what belongs to you, do not demand it back. Do to others as you would have them do to you.*

If you love those who love you what credit is that to you? Even sinners love those who love them. And if you do good to those who are good to you, what credit is that to you? Even sinners do that. And if you lend to those from whom you expect repayment, what credit is that to you? Even sinners lend to sinners expecting to be repaid in full. But love your enemies, do good to them, and lend to them without expecting to get anything back. Then your reward will be great, and you will be sons of the Most High, because he is kind to the ungrateful and wicked. Be merciful, just as your Father is merciful." (Luke 6:27-36 NIV)

LOVE - - - LOVE YOUR NEIGHBOR.

What is Love? In First Corinthians chapter 13 we read: *"Love is patient, Love is kind. It does not envy, it does not boast, it is not proud. It is not rude, it is not self-seeking, it is not easily angered, it keeps no record of wrongs. Love does not delight in evil but rejoices with the truth. It always protects, always trusts, always hopes, always perseveres. Love never fails ...."* (1 Corinthians 13:4-8a NIV)

So maybe now we can see a little how to love our neighbor as we love ourselves.

How To Show God How We Love Him?
1) **Accept God Free Gift of Salvation That He Gives Us In Love.**

"For God so loved the world that he gave his one and only Son, that whoever believes in him shall not perish but have eternal life." John 3:16 (NIV)

> 2) Worship the Lord With Gladness, Joyful Song, Thanksgiving and Praise.

"Shout for joy to the Lord, all the earth. Worship the Lord with gladness; come before him with joyful songs. Know that the Lord is God. It is he who made us, and we are his; we are his people, the sheep of his pasture. Enter his gates with thanksgiving and his courts with praise; give thanks to him and praise his name. For the Lord is Good and his love endures forever; his faithfulness continues through all generations." (Psalm 100 NIV)

But there is another way to show God we love Him. In Matthew 25 starting with verse 31 Jesus is telling us how it will be in the end. We read:

"When the Son of Man comes in his glory and all the angels with him, he will sit on his throne in heavenly glory. All the nations will be gathered before

him, and he will separate the people one from another as a shepherd separates the sheep from the goats. He will put the sheep on his right and the goats on his left.'

"Then the King will say to those on the right, 'Come, you who are blessed by my Father; take your inheritance, the Kingdom prepared for you since the creation of the world. For I was hungry and you gave me something to eat, I was thirsty and you gave me something to drink, I was a stranger and you invited me in. I needed clothes and you clothed me, I was sick and you looked after me, I was in prison and you came to visit me.'

"Then the righteous will answer him, Lord, when did we see you hungry and feed you, or thirsty and give you something to drink? When did we see you a stranger and invite you in, or needing clothes and clothe you? When did we see you sick or in prison and go to visit you?'

"The King will reply, I tell you the truth, whatever you did for one of the least of these brothers of mine, you did for me.'

"Then he will say to those on his left, 'Depart from me, you who are cursed, into the eternal fire prepared for the devil and his angels. For I was hungry

and you gave me nothing to drink, I was a stranger and you did not clothe me, I was sick and in prison and you did not look after me.'

"They also will answer, 'Lord, when did we see you hungry or thirsty or a stranger or needing clothes or sick or in prison, and did not help you?'

"He will reply, 'I tell you the truth, whatever you did not do for one of the least of these, you did not do for me.'

"Then they will go away to eternal punishment, but the righteous to eternal life." (Matt. 25:31-46 NIV)

3) So the Other Way We Can Show God How Much We Love Him is by Loving Others.

There are a couple of stories I would like to tell to help illustrate this principle. The first story goes on to say how Queen Victoria of England used to always like to dress up like the common people and go out around the country side. One day while she was out, a bad storm came up. Now if she did not look like royalty before the storm, she definitely did not look like it now. She went up to a house, all soaked and wet, and knocked on the door. A lady came to the door and the Queen asked if she could possibly come in to get out of the storm. Well the lady looked out at the storm for a minute and then said, "Well I guess you can come into the hallway here for a while."

The Queen came in the hallway and stood waiting for the storm to pass by. But the storm just kept on. The Queen knew that she had to be back at the palace for official business, so she asked the lady if she possibly had an umbrella that she could use to get home. She promised that she would have it back to her the next day.

The lady knew that she had two umbrellas in the closet. She had one new umbrella and one old one with several the wires sticking through it. She looked out the window at the storm and then looked at the pitiful wet Queen that she still did not recognize. Realizing that it would be dark soon she decided to give the old umbrella to the Queen. The Queen then hurried off into the storm.

The next day was a beautiful sunny day. The Queen's carriage pulled up in front of the lady's house and one of the Queen's guards came up to the house. The lady came to the door wondering why the Queen's carriage would be stopping at her house. The guard handed the lady the old umbrella and thanked her for her kindness and generosity to the Queen.

How would you feel if this lady was you and you realized that the wet, muddy, common looking woman

was the Queen and you did not give her your very best?

The other story takes place in the winter. It involves Sir Edwin Booth, a great Shakespearian actor. He was about to perform in one great play in England when his understudy came to him about 5 minutes before curtain time and said that no one was in the audience. Well at about one minute before curtain time six people came in and sat way in the back of the auditorium. It was dark in the back of the auditorium and no one could see who they were from the stage. Only six people showed up. This could have been because of the sleet and snow and below zero temperate outside.

The understudy went back to Booth and asked him not to go out with only six people and told him that it would be a disgrace for someone of his talent and class to go and perform for that small of group. Booth looked at his understudy and said, "I will perform for the King." It was just a type of saying in those days in England similar to "The show must go on".

Well the show did go on; Booth went out and did the best he could do. In fact he gave the best performance of his career, even though there were only six people in the back of the auditorium. He gave them all he had. Most people would have offered to give their money back because it would have not been worth it to perform just for six people.

The next day Sir Edwin Booth received an official letter commending him for his great performance. The letter was signed "The King of England".

LOVE GOD and LOVE YOUR NEIGHBOR

LOVE is the key. It is what Jesus is all about. It is what the Bible is all about.

"For God so loved the world that he gave his one and only Son, that whoever believes in him shall not perish but have eternal life." John 3:16 (NIV)

It is up to us now. Do we love God with all our heart and with all our soul and with our entire mind, and do we love others as ourselves? Have we <u>accepted</u> God Free Gift of Salvation that He Offers Us In Love?

IS GOD OUR FATHER?

Is God our Father? Are we children of God? Am I a child of God? **John 3:16** (NIV) states: ***"For God so loved the world that he gave his one and only son, that whoever believes in him shall not perish but have eternal life."***

What does it mean to "**believe in Him**"? What does it mean to **believe**?

I think that Satan has got a lot of people fooled. I think that today there are a lot of people that may be mistaken on whether they are a child of God or not. I want all reading this to examine themselves. Ask God to help you examine your life by the power of the Holy Spirit in Jesus' Name. Pray to God. Read His word and find out the Truth before it is too late. Ask; "Am I a child of God or am I fooling myself?"

Many repeat the Apostle's Creed each week in church, but does that make them children of God? Does believing that all of the statements of the Apostle's Creed are true make us children of God? Does just believing the "facts" about Jesus' Birth, death and resurrection make us children of God? Does just believing that Jesus Christ was and is the Son of God make us children of God? If just knowing the "facts" about Jesus makes us children of God, then what about the demons? In **Luke 8:26-** we read about the healing of the demon possessed man, that shouted at the top of his voice; ***"What do you want with me, Jesus, Son of the most high God?"*** This demon inside that man knew the "facts" about Jesus. He knew the power Jesus has over all creation, both physical and spiritual.

The Bible tells us:

How Jesus cast out demons.

How Jesus healed those that were deaf and mute.

How Jesus calmed the sea.

How Jesus turned water into wine.

How Jesus healed the crippled.

How Jesus fed thousands with just a few loaves of bread and a few fish.

How Jesus healed the blind.

How Jesus healed every disease and sickness among the people.

How Jesus raised the dead.

Yes, the Bible is clear that Jesus, the Son of God, has all power and authority over creation. Are we saved, are we children of God by knowing and accepting these "facts"?

There are some people who have gone to seminary and/or Bible School for years to know the facts of the Bible that have never met God <u>personally</u>. They have never become a child of God. There are all kinds of people from all walks of life that believe in the "facts" of Jesus but they don't have the Father Child relationship with God. They may really think that because of knowing the "facts" of Jesus that they are children of God. They think God is their Father.

Jesus says in **Matthew 7:15-21 (NIV)**, **"*Watch out for false prophets. They come to you in sheep's clothing, but inwardly they are ferocious wolves. By their fruit you will recognize them. Do people pick grapes from thorn bushes, or figs from thistles?***

Likewise every good tree bears good fruit, but a bad tree bears bad fruit. A good tree cannot bear bad fruit, and a bad tree cannot bear good fruit. Every tree that does not bear good fruit is cut down and thrown into the fire. Thus, by their fruit you will recognize them. Not everyone who says to me, Lord, Lord will enter the kingdom of heaven, but only he who does the will of my Father who is in heaven."

Now I know what some of you reading this are thinking now. "Salvation is a free gift. It is not by works." I agree with you 100%. Salvation is a free gift. **Ephesians 2:8-9 (NIV)** says, *"For it is by grace you have been saved, through faith - and this not from yourselves, it is the gift of God - not by works, so that no one can boast."* This is where most people stop reading. But let us read on through verse 10. *"For we are God's workmanship, created in Christ Jesus to do good works, which God prepared in advance for us to do."*

Let's get back to meaning of believe. **John 3:16 (NIV)** states: *"For God so loved the world that he gave his one and only son, that whoever believes in him shall not perish but have eternal life."* What is this believing we have to do to have eternal life? What is this belief? It can't just know some facts. I think that this belief could be best defined by telling you a story that I heard that happened a while back at Niagara Falls.

There was a tight rope walker who had his tight rope strung across the falls while a great number of spectators had gathered there to watch him cross the falls. This man walked across the falls on his tiny little tight rope. All who watched knew that one wrong move could mean the end of his life. That man walked on that rope with ease. He walked with confidence across the falls and then back again.

Then the man asked the spectators if they *believed* that he could take a wheelbarrow across the falls on the tight rope. A few in the crowd said that they *believed* he could. Well, this man took a wheelbarrow, with the tire off of the rim, and placed it empty on the rope. The man then started out across the falls. He went across and back again with what still looks as easy as without the wheelbarrow.

The man then asked the crowd of spectators if they *believed* that he could place 200 pounds of brick in the wheelbarrow and cross the falls. This time more of the crowd shouted, "Yes, we *believe* that you can do it!" The tight rope walker then carefully placed 200 pounds of brick into the wheelbarrow and walked across the falls, still with ease.

The crowd was cheering as they watched the great task that the tight rope walker done. They all *believed* that this man must be the very best tight rope walker ever. The tight rope walker then asked the crowd, "Do you *believe* that I could put a man into the wheelbarrow and go across the falls?" The entire crowd now shouted together, "Yes, we *believe* that you can do it!" The tight rope walker noticed one young man up front of the crowd that was all excited and shouted with the others that he *believed* in the tight rope walker being able to do it. He asked the young man, "Sir, you seem to *believe* so much, I want you to climb in the wheelbarrow." As soon as the words lefts his mouth, the young man started turning a pale white and then turned and ran away.

Did he really believe? Do we really believe in Jesus? Do we believe in Jesus enough to put our lives on the line if God asks us to? The Bible tells us that Jesus only did the Will of the Father. Jesus obeyed even when that meant death on the cross. We are called to follow Jesus. Maybe we will not have to suffer death for Him, but what if we one day are asked to put our lives on the line? Are we willing to do God's Will no matter what? Remember in Matthew we read, **"only he who does the will of my Father will enter the kingdom of heaven."**

Are we children of God? Is God our Father? **Mark 3:35 (NIV)** we find Jesus saying, *"Whoever does God's will is my brother and my sister and mother."* Are we in that family? Are we doing God's Will? Do we really believe with the kind of faith that is willing to do whatever God asks us to do? Are we willing to climb into the wheelbarrow?

<u>Will you surrender your life to God today?</u> Decide to give Him your life unconditionally today. Let God have complete control of your life, today. Climb in His wheelbarrow, today. **2 Corinthians 6:2 (NIV)** says, *"...now is the time of God's favor, now is the day of salvation."* Please don't put off the most important decision of your life until tomorrow. Tomorrow may not come for you. **James 4:14 (NIV)** says, *"...you do not even know what will happen tomorrow. What is life? You are a mist that appears for a little while and then vanishes."*

UNCONDITIONAL SURRENDER CAN MEAN ULTIMATE WINNING!

I would like to start with just a few verses from the Bible. But before you read them ask God to speak to you through His Word and this message to make a difference in your life and in the lives of those around you. Stop now and ask God to speak to you personally. Ask Him to reveal the message He wants you to get. Ask Him to make you an Ultimate Winner.

Matthew 28:18 - 20 (NIV)

"...All authority in heaven and on earth has been given to me. Therefore go and make disciples of all nations, baptizing them in the name of the Father and of the Son and of the Holy Spirit, and teaching them to

obey everything I have commanded you. And surely I am with you always, to the very end of the age."

Acts 1:8 (NIV)

"But you will receive power when the Holy Spirit comes on you; and you will be my witnesses in Jerusalem, and in all Judea and Samaria, and to the ends of the earth."

2 Timothy 3:1 - 5 (NIV)

"But mark this: There will be terrible times in the last days. People will be lovers of themselves, lovers of money, boastful, proud, abusive, disobedient to their parents, ungrateful, unholy, without love, unforgiving, slanderous, without self-control, brutal, not lovers of God - having a form of godliness but denying its power. Have nothing to do with them."

Revelation 3:5 - 6 (NIV)

"I know your deeds, that you are neither cold nor hot. I wish you were either one or the other! So, because you are lukewarm - neither hot nor cold - I am about to spit you out of my mouth."

Hebrews 13:8 (NIV)

"Jesus Christ is the same yesterday and today and forever."

Revelation 3:20 (NIV)

"Here I am! I stand at the door and knock. If anyone hears my voice and opens the door, I will come in and eat with him, and he with me."

Matthew 5:6 (NIV)

"Blessed are those who hunger and thirst for righteousness, for they will be filled."

God has called us to be disciples of Jesus Christ. We are to be missionaries and ministers of the full gospel of Jesus Christ today in the places that God has placed us. God has given the Holy Spirit to be with us and to empower us to carry out His Will. The mission of In Him Ministries is to *"Help You Reach Your Full Potential In Messiah!"*. This should be the desire of all who have called on the name of the Lord Jesus to be their Lord and Savior. God wants to dwell in us and work through us today with the same fullness of power seen in the New Testament. We can't do the work without the presence and power of God in us. We have to surrender unconditionally to God's Holy Spirit to allow our full potential In Christ to come forth. It is a daily surrender. And it is God working in and through us that will make the difference. The walls that separate His children must come down. The Love of God must flow in and through us. This can only be done when each one of us totally unconditionally surrender to God.

God is calling His children to a real, on fire, personal relationship with Him. He is calling His children to seek Him with their whole heart, mind, soul, and strength. He is calling His children to hunger and thirst after His righteousness. It is time to get rid of all the hidden sins that we have been carrying around. It is time to become pure in His sight. It is not a time to continue to play religion or get religious. It is a time to get real with a personal relationship with God. It is time to allow God complete control of our lives. It is time to stand in His presence. It is time to walk in Him. It is time to listen to and obey Him. We are going to have to surrender completely to Him and allow Him to do whatever is needed in order to get us right with Him. It is a time to no longer be lukewarm and to just play church. It is a time to get "hot" and start being the Church. It is a time of renewal. It is a time of refreshing. It is a time to really get to know God personally and intimately, not just to know about Him. God is calling His children to a new depth of total surrender, total obedience, and total power. We are at the edge of a great awakening that the world has never seen. We are at the beginning of a great outpouring of His Holy Spirit upon His children that will make the miracles in the Bible come alive. As we spend more time seeking Him and being in His presence, His anointing will also come and His power will work through the people called by His name. The Church, the real Church, will come alive again with mighty power. His children will awaken to the times and will be able to do mighty things, in Christ, as they surrender completely to Him.

Yes, God has called us and is still calling us to be disciples of Jesus Christ. We are to be missionaries and ministers of the full gospel of Jesus Christ today in the places that God has placed us. God has given the Holy Spirit to be with us and to empower us to carry out His Will. God wants to dwell in us and work through us today with the same fullness of power seen in the New Testament. We can't do the work without being in Him. We have to surrender unconditionally to God's Holy Spirit to allow our full potential In Christ to come forth. It is a daily surrender. And it is God working in and through us that will make the difference. Unconditional Surrender to God will make us

Ultimate Winners In Christ. Are you ready to take the step of total surrender to God today? Start your daily surrender today and move ahead to reach your full potential in Christ.

I would like to close with a prayer from Benny Hinn's book "THE ANOINTING", copyrighted 1992 and published in Nashville, Tennessee, by Thomas Nelson, Inc.

"Father, I surrender to You completely now. I yield everything to You - my body, my soul, and my spirit, my family, my job, my finances, my weaknesses, my strengths, my past, my present, and my future, everything I am, for all eternity. I ask You, Lord, to give me a repentant heart for all the things I've done to grieve You, all my sins, my iniquities, my coldness of heart, and my lack of trust, I ask You to empower me to turn around, to go the other way, the way that pleases You. Holy Spirit, I welcome you into my life right now. I praise You and love You. I ask You to help me receive the things I've asked for from the Father through Jesus. Help me to come into fellowship and communion with You, for I really don't know how to myself. Make me fully aware of Your presence and enable me to hear Your voice. I promise to obey. Lord Jesus, anoint me with the Holy Spirit as I obey and

learn. Give me Your power to touch those around me and those You will bring across my path. Show me what to do next. And help me never to neglect Your fellowship. I pray in the name of Jesus my Lord. Amen. "

ARE WE WILLING TO DO WHATEVER HE ASKS?

My father was a pastor for thirty years. One thing that he loved doing was his children's sermons. Every Sunday during the morning service he would have a special time when all the children were asked to come up. They would come up to the front of the church and gathering around him and then he would tell them a very simple story. In that story would be a "nugget of truth" that was full of some aspect of God. Then he would always try to have some little treat for each of them to take with them as they went back to their seat. Sometimes it was a little toy, a piece of candy or a piece of gum. They always look forward to this time. It was their special time with their pastor. And it was his very special time with them. My father seemed to always have them on his mind throughout the week. I can remember often being in a store with him when he would see something he thought his children would like to have and he would try to think of an illustration to use with it to teach a "nugget of truth" to them.

There was one children's sermon he used that I feel I need to tell to you today. He often used this very early after coming to a new church. This was often before the children really got to know him deeply. In this sermon he would pull out a silver dollar and hold it for all to see. This was not one of the newer silver dollars the size of a quarter. This was one of those big ones that were worth more than face value. He would ask them if they knew what it was. Then he would say that he wanted to give it to one of them today. They would all say, "Me! Me!" Then he would tell them, "I will give it to the one willing to do whatever I tell them to do."

He let them know that in order to receive it they would have to be willing to do anything he asked. This always cut the number of children wanting the silver dollar down. Maybe there would only be one or two children now saying that they were willing and trusted my father enough to do whatever he said. He would then ask again, "Are you sure that you will do whatever I ask you to do?" Sometimes he would give examples of some of the things

51

he just might ask. Finally only one would be left to do whatever my father asked.

The child would come and stand before my father, looking up into his eyes waiting for instruction. My father might ask one more time if they were sure they were willing to do anything asked. Then as he would hold the silver dollar up for all to see, he would say, *"Reach up and take it"*. He never held it out of their reach but he always made them stretch out their hand in order to receive the dollar.

He then would tell them that God wants to bless them too. Maybe not with money but He has gifts for all of His children. He wants to give to those who will trust Him and who are willing to obey Him. He then gave the example of eternal life through Jesus. It was a free gift, we just have to reach up, trusting Him and receive it.

God, the Father, is not limited in the number of silver dollars He has as my father was. He has more than enough for everyone. He wants to give all of His children precious gifts today. Sometimes we may not even know what the gift is. But just as my father always had the children on his mind and was always looking for something to give them, so does our Heavenly Father.

The Father is pouring out His Spirit to many of His children today. He is asking you to be willing to receive what He has for you. You may not even know the value of what He is giving out, just like many of the children did not really know the value of a real old silver dollar. But we have to trust Him in order to receive His gift.

Many of the children at my father's churches would have kicked themselves for not being the one to go up and receive. But worse than that, there was one time, at one church that my father went to, that no one was willing to go up and do whatever my father asked. No one received the silver dollar that day, nor did my father repeat the same opportunity to that same group again.

Do not let any of us reading this message be one that does not trust God enough to just reach up to Him and say, "I don't know for sure what you have for me, and I don't know what you would have me to do, but I willing to do whatever you would have me do in order to receive whatever you have for me.

The following is a prayer that you might like to adopt as your own:

"Father, I ask forgiveness for my past sins. I ask forgiveness for not putting my whole trust in You. I ask forgiveness for not really, completely, surrendering everything to You. I reach up to You now and I gaze into Your eyes and I ask for Your Will to be done.

Whatever You want, I will do. Wherever You say go, I will go. Whatever You have for me, I accept."

"Lord, produce the fruit of Your Spirit within me. Lord, God, give me a real, on fire, personal relationship with You. You are calling me to seek You with my whole heart, mind, soul, and strength. You are calling me to hunger and thirst after Your righteousness. It is time to get rid of all the hidden sins that I have been carrying around. It is time for me to become pure in Your sight. It is not a time for me to play religion or get religious. It is a time for me to get a real personal relationship with You, Lord Jesus. It is time to allow Your Holy Spirit complete control of my life. It is time to stand in Your presence. It is time to walk in Your Spirit. It is time to listen to and obey Your Spirit. I am going to surrender completely to You now and allow You to do whatever is needed in my life in order to get me right with You. It is a time for me to no longer be lukewarm. It is a time for me to get "hot" and start being what You have called me to be. It is a time of renewal. It is a time of refreshing. It is a time for me to really get to know You personally and intimately, not just to know about You."

"Father God, I believe You are calling all of Your children to a new depth of total surrender. You are calling us all to total obedience, and total power. We are at the edge of a great awakening that the world has never seen before. We are at the beginning of a great outpouring of Your Holy Spirit upon Your children that will make the miracles in the Bible come alive. As we spend more time seeking You, O Lord, and being in Your presence, may Your anointing come upon us and Your power work through the people called by Your Holy Name. May the Church come alive again with mighty power. May the walls that have separated Your children by different groups come down. May the sin of anger and resentment between our brothers and sisters come down. May the sin of pride, the sin of thinking that we are better than our brothers or sisters come down. May we join with the prayer of Jesus, "As You are - so let us be one". Join us together in the power of Your Spirit."

"Yes, Father, light the fire in us again! Pour out Your Spirit upon us, O Lord. Let us receive Your mercy. Send Your refiner's fire to purify our hearts and cleanse us. Let Your Glory fall upon us. Let Your kingdom come. Let Your will be done. Let the whole world see on earth the glory of Your Son. May your children awake to the times and be able to do mighty things, in Christ, as we each surrender completely to You now."

Matthew 7:9-11 (NIV)

"Which of you, if his son asks for bread, will give him a stone? Or if he asks for a fish, will give him a snake? If you, then, though you are evil, know how to give good gifts to your children, how much more will your Father in heaven give good gifts to those who ask him!"

Acts 2:17-18, & 21 (NIV)

"In the last days, God says, I will pour out my Spirit on all people. Your sons and daughters will prophesy, your young men will see visions, your old men will dream dreams. Even on my servants, both men and women, I will pour out my Spirit in those days, and they will prophesy."

"And everyone who calls on the name of the Lord will be saved."

A TIME FOR TRUE UNITY IN HIM

Many times we see our church or our denomination as the only one that is right. We often see our little body as the best and most important. But we need to see it the way God sees it. I heard a minister once say that the Body of Christ is like a river. In that river are many different currents, but they all are of the same water and make up the whole river. It takes all kinds of currents to make the river what it is. Just because the current we are in at the moment is not like another part of the river, that doesn't make the other currents not part of the whole river. We need to recognize that we are all of the River of God and allow Him to stir the currents the way He wishes. We need to see the whole river as one moving living body of water. Let us read over some words from the Bible. As we read them, ask God to open our eyes and our hearts so that He can work in and through us to reveal His Will for us. Help us so that we can become One Body in Him.

(1 Corinthians 12:12-20 NIV) "The body is a unit, though it is made up of many parts; and though all its parts are many, they form one body. So it is with Christ. For we were all baptized by one Spirit into one body - whether Jews or Greeks, slave or free - and we were all given the one Spirit to drink."

"Now the body is not made up of one part but of many. If the foot should say, "Because I am not a hand, I do not belong to the body," it would not for that reason cease to be part of the body. And if the ear should say, "Because I am not an eye, I do not belong to the body," It would not for that reason cease to be part of the body. If the whole body were an eye, where would the sense of hearing be? If the whole body were an ear, where would the sense of smell be? But in fact God has arranged the parts in the body, every one of them, just as he wanted them to be. If they were all one part, where would the body be? As it is, there are many parts, but one body."

(Romans 12:4-5 NIV) "Just as each of us has one body with many members, and these members do not all have the same function, so in Christ we who are many

form one body, and each member belongs to all the others."

(Ephesians 4:2-6 NIV) "Be completely humble and gentle; be patient, bearing with one another in love. Make every effort to keep the unity of the Spirit through the bond of peace. There is one body and one Spirit - just as you were called to one hope when you were called - one Lord, one faith, one baptism; one God and Father of all, who is over all and through all and in all."

(John 13:35 NIV) "By this all men will know that you are my disciples, if you love one another."

(1 Corinthians 13:4-7 NIV) "Love is patient, love is kind. It does not envy, it does not boast, it is not proud. It is not rude, it is not self-seeking, it is not easily angered, it keeps no record of wrongs. Love does not delight in evil but rejoices with the truth. It always protects, always trust, always hopes, always perseveres."

(Ephesians 4:29-32 NIV) "Do not let any unwholesome talk come out of your mouths, but only what is helpful

for building others up according to their needs, that it may benefit those who listen. And do not grieve the Holy Spirit of God, with whom you were sealed for the day of redemption. Get rid of all bitterness, rage and anger, brawling and slander, along with every form of malice. Be kind and compassionate to one another, forgiving each other, just as in Christ God forgave you."

(Colossians 3:12-14 NIV) "Therefore, as God's chosen people, holy and dearly loved, clothe yourselves with compassion, kindness, humility, gentleness and patience. Bear with each other and forgive whatever grievances you may have against one another. Forgive as the Lord forgave you. And over all these virtues put on love, which binds them all together in perfect unity."

(1 John 2:10-11 NIV) "Whoever loves his brother lives in the light, and there is nothing in him to make him stumble. But whoever hates his brother is in the darkness and walks around in the darkness; he does not know where he is going, because the darkness has blinded him."

(1 John 4:20-21 NIV) "If anyone says, "I love God," yet hates his brother, he is a liar. For anyone who does not love his brother, whom he has seen, cannot love God, whom he has not seen. And he has given us this command: Whoever loves God must also love his brother."

Many people are praying for revival to come on their church. Many are praying for God to bless them or their little group. We need to get God's picture on this. Tony Evans basically said at Promise Keepers in Atlanta Georgia in 1995 that God will not send revival to just part of His Body. He will not send it to just a white church or a black church, to a Methodist church or a Baptist church, or to any other part of His Body. He will only (true revival) send it to His whole Body.

We must let all the different types of walls, which we have built up, to come down. We need to love all of our brothers and sisters. It does not matter what race or denomination we are. It does not matter what current of the river they are from. It does not matter what happened in the past that may have hurt us and caused a wall to go up. We need to forgive. We need to love. We need to rise up as the whole Body of Christ. We need to focus on God and His Will for His Body for the future, not on our differences and our failures of the past. Let us all repent, forgive each other, and reach out in love to one another and break down all the walls that we have allowed Satan to erect between us. Please don't take this message wrong. Don't let this message become another wall. I am just as guilty, if not more so, for allowing many different walls to go up. Please forgive me. Now is the time to come together in the Spirit of Christ. Let us realize if one part suffers, every part suffers with it. Let us pray for each other for God to bless our brothers and sisters more that ourselves. The time has come to join with other Christians and Ministries to complete the Great Commission. We must join together from different denominations and ethnic backgrounds to become <u>One in Christ</u>. We all are part of the Body of Christ and we need to work together to complete His Great Commission. All of us have a different function and purpose within the Body. Each of us can reach some person that another cannot reach. By working together we can complete the Great Commission in our lifetime. We must tear down the walls. We must forgive. We must Love.

I have quoted two songs that help say what I believe is God's Will in this matter of the walls that we have allowed to be built within His Body.

LET THE WALLS FALL DOWN

(John and Anne Barbour, and Bill Batstone)

Let the walls fall down   (let the walls fall down)
Let the walls fall down   (let the walls fall down)
Let the walls fall down   (let the walls fall down)
By His love, let the walls fall down.

One by one, we're drawn together
One by one, to Jesus' side
One in Him, we'll live forever
Strangers He has reconciled.

In His love, no walls between us
In His love a common ground
Kneeling at the cross of Jesus
All our pride comes tumbling down

1993 Maranatha Praise, Inc.
Words typed from Promise Keepers CD.

BREAK DIVIDING WALLS

(David Ruis)

There is a place of commanded blessing
Where brethren in unity dwell
A place where anointing oil is flowing
Where we live as one

You have called us to be a body
You have called us as friends
Joined together in the bond of the Spirit
Unto the end

Father we join with the prayer of Jesus
As You are so let us be one
Joined together in unity and purpose
All for the love of Your Son

We will break dividing walls, we will break dividing walls
We will break dividing walls, in the name of Your Son
We will break dividing walls, we will break dividing walls
And we will be one

<u>Words typed from Vineyard Music Group,</u>
<u>"DAVID RUIS, Break Dividing Walls"</u>

Lord God, make the walls that have separated Your children by different groups come down. Forgive us Lord for our sins. Forgive us for the sin of anger and resentment between our brothers and sisters. Forgive us of the sin of pride, the sin of thinking that we are better than our brothers or sisters. Forgive us for not loving our brothers and sisters as we should have. Forgive us for not asking You to Bless our brothers and sisters more than us. May we join now with the prayer of Jesus, "As You are - so let us be One". Join us together in the power of Your Spirit. Lord, You bring true unity in us today.

~ In Jesus' Name ~

MAKING A DIFFERENCE BY FORGIVING

Parable of the Unforgiving Servant

(Matthew 18:21-35 NIV)

"Then Peter came to Jesus and asked, "Lord, how many times shall I forgive my brother or sister who sins against me? Up to seven times?"

Jesus answered, "I tell you, not seven times, but seventy-seven times.

"Therefore, the kingdom of heaven is like a king who wanted to settle accounts with his servants. As he began the settlement, a man who owed him ten thousand bags of gold was brought to him. Since he was not able to pay, the master ordered that he and his wife and his children and all that he had be sold to repay the debt.

"At this the servant fell on his knees before him. 'Be patient with me,' he begged, 'and I will pay back

everything.' The servant's master took pity on him, canceled the debt and let him go.

"But when that servant went out, he found one of his fellow servants who owed him a hundred silver coins. He grabbed him and began to choke him. 'Pay back what you owe me!' he demanded.

"His fellow servant fell to his knees and begged him, 'Be patient with me, and I will pay it back.'

"But he refused. Instead, he went off and had the man thrown into prison until he could pay the debt. When the other servants saw what had happened, they were outraged and went and told their master everything that had happened.

"Then the master called the servant in. 'You wicked servant,' he said, 'I canceled all that debt of yours because you begged me to. Shouldn't you have had mercy on your fellow servant just as I had on you?' In anger his master handed him over to the jailers to be tortured, until he should pay back all he owed.

"This is how my heavenly Father will treat each of you unless you forgive your brother or sister from your heart."

Forgiveness: We all need it. And we all need to give it.

Today we are going to look at several principles from God's Word concerning "Forgiveness" and then see what we need to do to in order to put these principles into practice so that we can make a difference.

Pat Robertson says "Unforgiveness" is a particularly sin that blocks access to the kingdom and to its marvelous power. I believe that by looking at this parable of the Unforgiving Servant and looking at these other verses we will be able to realize the importance's of true forgiveness.

(Others Scriptures on Forgiveness)
Matt. 18:18 *(bind on earth, bound in heaven)*,
Matt. 6:12 *(Lord's Prayer & forgiving)*,
Matt. 6:14 & 15 *(forgive others and receive forgiveness)*,
Ps. 103:12 *(When God forgives He removes it as far as the east is from the west)*,
Matt. 5:23 & 24, *(it's your responsibility to make the first move)*
1 Cor. 11:27-29 *(examine ourselves, be sure we are not unworthy)*,
1 John 1:9 *(if we confess ours sins, He is faithful and just and will forgive us our sins and purify us from all unrighteousness)*

If we want to make a difference for the Kingdom of God then we too must forgive. There are four different ways this forgiveness needs to be directed in order to insure we cover all possible unforgiveness within our hearts.

1) THE FIRST PERSON WE HAVE TO "FORGIVE" IS OURSELVES.

More people lack forgiveness for themselves than toward anybody else. They are unwilling to forgive themselves and to recognize what God says in *(Psalm 103:12 NIV), "As far as the east is from the west, so far has He removed our transgressions from us"*.

If you are born again, if you are new creature in Christ, then this is true of you. Your sins have been removed as far as the east is from the west. We cannot let Satan keep bringing up those things that God has removed. If we don't forgive ourselves, we will never be able to reach the full potential God has for us.

2) THE SECOND PERSON WE HAVE TO "FORGIVE", IF WE HAVE BITTERNESS IN US, IS GOD HIMSELF.

People are too quick to blame God for so many problems that come their way. If we blame God, even if it is subconsciously done, it will cause a deep seated resentment in our live. We cannot be resentful toward God and experience kingdom power flowing in our life. We have to get rid of any bitterness toward God. We need to ask Him if we are blaming Him for anything or any situation, past or present. Then we need to forgive Him and ask forgiveness.

3) THE THIRD PERSON WE HAVE TO "FORGIVE" IS A MEMBER OF OUR FAMILY. *(Home and Church Family)*

Often tension, misunderstandings, and resentments will develop within a family. Often we will write them off as just a fact of life and we will not really forgive the ones closest to us. On the surface things may look O.K., but deep down there is resentment growing within us. This is often why we have broken homes and church splits today. The spirit of unforgiveness is from Satan. We have to truly forgive our family members completely in order to allow God's power to freely flow in and through us. (Matt. 5:23 & 24 we are to make the first move)

4) FINALLY, THERE HAS TO BE FORGIVENESS FOR ANYBODY ELSE WHO HAS EVER DONE ANYTHING AGAINST US.

Anybody! It may be that the resentment is justified. It may be that the person has done a very evil, terrible thing to you. You may have every legal right to hold a grudge against them. **But** if you want to see kingdom life and power flow through you, then forgiveness is a must.

Jesus showed us the ultimate example of forgiveness when they nailed Him to the cross He prayed, ***"Father forgive them, for they do not know what they are doing." (Luke 23:34)***

Let us now spend a few minutes praying for God to reveal any unforgiveness in us. Then pray to forgive Yourself, God, Family, and All Others so that we can make a difference for God today and forever.

YOU CAN MAKE A DIFFERENCE
BY FORGIVING

HOW TO MAKE A DIFFERENCE:

WALK THE TALK

(1 John 3:1-7 NIV) *"See what great love the Father has lavished on us, that we should be called children of God! And that is what we are! The reason the world does not know us is that it did not know him. Dear friends, now we are children of God, and what we will be has not yet been made known. But we know that when Christ appears, we shall be like him, for we shall see him as he is. All who have this hope in him purify themselves, just as he is pure."*

"Everyone who sins breaks the law; in fact, sin is lawlessness. But you know that he appeared so that he might take away our sins. And in him is no sin. No one who lives in him keeps on sinning. No one who continues to sin has either seen him or known him."

"Dear children, do not let anyone lead you astray. The one who does what is right is righteous, just as he is righteous."

Today we are going to look at one way the early church made a difference. They "Walked the Talk". They turned the world right side up. Today many see Christian's as hypocrites. They say one thing but do another.

What are some reasons for not coming to church? People are not interested in just hearing the Word, they want and need to see it in actions and deeds. No more religious hypocrites! People want to see people like Billy Graham, Mother Teresa, & Jimmy Carter with Integrity!

They want to see people of Integrity. That's what we must be if we are going to make a difference in our world. That's what Holiness is. It is Walking the Talk. When we do what we say, people will listen. If we don't, they won't.

Today we are going to look at three ways that we can learn to Walk the Talk.

1) GET SERIOUS ABOUT LIVING UP TO YOUR POTENTIAL.

(read verse 2) *"Dear friends, now we are children of God, and what we will be has not yet been made known. But we know that when Christ appears, we shall be like him, for we shall see him as he is."*

We are children of God. As Christians, God is in us.

"I can do all things through Christ..." Realize You Can Make A Difference. You Are Designed To Make A Difference. Realize that You are who God says You are.

Here is a story as an example of the "I can do all things..." Way back in the county on a dirt road a car got stuck in a ditch. While the driver was trying to get the car out, a farmer came along with a mule. Farmer with a old, swayback, almost blind mule named "DUSTY". The farmer as the driver of the car if he wanted help to car get out of the ditch by having Dusty pull it out. The driver side yes, he could use whatever help he could get. The farmer hooked a rope to the car and then he yelled out, "Pull Buck....Pull Clyde...Pull Dusty. And Dusty pulled the car out of the ditch.

The man asked a question? *If your mule is name DUSTY, why did you first yell, "Pull Buck and Pull Clyde"?*

The Farmer answered? *"Dusty is old and doesn't see too good, and doesn't have much confidence.* <u>**If he thought he had to do all the work himself, he'd never even try**</u>*."*

Now some of us can maybe relate to the old mule to a certain degree. If we thought we had to do all the work ourselves we may not even try as well. But we are not along! Christ is In Us! With Him we can do all things.

2) SPEND TIME ALONE WITH JESUS

(1 John 3:6) says;

"No one who lives in him keeps on sinning. No one who continues to sin has either seen him or known him." "No one who lives in Him keeps on sinning..."

If you want power over sin, the ability to live a holy life, able to walk the talk, we must spend time with Jesus. How are you spending or investing your time? What are you putting into your mind? What you put in is often what you get out. You become like that you put in. Spend time putting the good stuff in and you will get the good stuff out. Spend time with Jesus. Pray, Bible Study, Fellowship with Believers, Walk with Jesus. Let Jesus be your Best Friend or "Your Mate" as Clark Taylor and Darryl McGavin from Down Under in Australia would call Him. Spend time with Jesus and you will become more like Him.

3) LOOK FOR THE CHANCE TO DO GOOD

(1 John 3:7) says;

"Dear children, do not let anyone lead you astray. The one who does what is right is righteous, just as he is righteous."

"He who does what is right is righteous..." They went around doing good. John Wesley said, *"Do all the good you can, by all the means you can, in all the ways you can, to all the people you can, as long as you can."*

Action speaks louder than words. There comes a point when Action is needed. In **James 2:26** says **"...faith without works is dead." Ephesians 2:10** says **...we were "created in Christ Jesus to do good works..."**

WE NEED TO WALK THE TALK

Remember the example of Good Samaritan in *Luke 10:25-37 (NIV) "On one occasion an expert in the law stood up to test Jesus. "Teacher," he asked, "what must I do to inherit eternal life?"*

"What is written in the Law?" he replied. "How do you read it?"

He answered, "'Love the Lord your God with all your heart and with all your soul and with all your strength and with all your mind'; and, 'Love your neighbor as yourself.'"

"You have answered correctly," Jesus replied. "Do this and you will live."

But he wanted to justify himself, so he asked Jesus, "And who is my neighbor?"

In reply Jesus said: "A man was going down from Jerusalem to Jericho, when he was attacked by robbers. They stripped him of his clothes, beat him and went away, leaving him half dead. A priest happened to be going down the same road, and when he saw the man, he passed by on the other side. So too, a Levite, when he came to the place and saw him, passed by on the other side. But a Samaritan, as he traveled, came where the man was; and when he saw him, he took pity on him. He went to him and bandaged his wounds, pouring on oil and wine. Then he put the man on his own donkey, brought him to an inn and took care of him. The next day he took out two denarii and gave them to the innkeeper. 'Look after him,' he said, 'and *when I return, I will reimburse you for any extra expense you may have.'*

"Which of these three do you think was a neighbor to the man who fell into the hands of robbers?"

The expert in the law replied, "The one who had mercy on him." Jesus told him, "Go and do likewise."

There was a Man dying...3 men pass by...2 Religious and they do nothing....They might have been late for religious activity. The Samaritan stopped, had compassion, helped, paid, and walked the talk.

TO REVIEW:

1) **GET SERIOUS ABOUT LIVING UP TO YOUR POTENTIAL.**

2) **SPEND TIME ALONE WITH JESUS**

3) **LOOK FOR THE CHANCE TO DO GOOD**

YOU CAN MAKE A DIFFERENCE IN OUR WORLD TODAY BY LEARNING TO WALK THE TALK

HOW TO MAKE A DIFFERENCE: LEARNING TO LOVE

(1 John 3:16-24 NIV)

"This is how we know what love is: Jesus Christ laid down his life for us. And we ought to lay down our lives for our brothers and sisters. If anyone has material possessions and sees a brother or sister in need but has no pity on them, how can the love of God be in that person? Dear children, let us not love with words or speech but with actions and in truth."

"This is how we know that we belong to the truth and how we set our hearts at rest in his presence: If our hearts condemn us, we know that God is greater than our hearts, and he knows everything. Dear friends, if our hearts do not condemn us, we have confidence before God and receive from him anything

we ask, because we keep his commands and do what pleases him. And this is his command: to believe in the name of his Son, Jesus Christ, and to love one another as he commanded us. The one who keeps God's commands lives in him, and he in them. And this is how we know that he lives in us: We know it by the Spirit he gave us."

Today we are going to look at another way the early church made a difference. They **"Learned to Love".**
Often when people read the Bible they are looking for loopholes. People often look for some little loophole to justify their actions.

When it come to the command to "Love one another", Jesus didn't just stop with the word "love" without explaining it greater because he knew that we would look for a loophole. In John 13:34 Jesus says to "Love one another as I have loved you..." and then He says, "...all men will know that you are my disciples, if you love one another."

God takes love seriously. He loves us and He expects us to love one another. The early church made a difference in their world was because they loved one another. We cannot make a difference in this world if we don't love others. For every person that comes to Christ out of thought or reason, 99 will just be loved into the Kingdom.

What is love? *(1 Corinthians 13:4-7 NIV) "Love is patient, love is kind. It does not envy, it does not boast, it is not proud. It does not dishonor others, it is not self-seeking, it is not easily angered, it keeps no record of wrongs. Love does not delight in evil but rejoices with the truth. It always protects, always trusts, always hopes, always perseveres."*

The difference you make in your world will be determined by primarily one factor: how much you love. How do we measure love? John tells us in *(1 John 3:18 NIV) "Dear children, let us not love with words or tongue but with actions and in truth."*

The difference you make will be determined by how much you love. How much love is determined by how much you do. Love is something you do. Love is not a feeling. It is a commitment to action. Love is an action. It is something you do.

How do we learn to love as Jesus loves? What does that involve? What can we do to grow more loving toward others?

We are going to look at three ways to grow in love.

1) OPEN YOUR EYES   (Vs 17)

In the story of the Good Samaritan, A lawyer came to Jesus and asked what he must do to inherit eternal life. Jesus confirmed that the law to him by saying, **"Love God with all your heart, and love your neighbor as yourself."** The lawyer looked for a loophole and asked **"Who is my neighbor?"** Jesus tells the story of the Good Samaritan that our neighbor is anyone we have the opportunity to help.

Love requires that we open our eyes. Look for opportunity to do good. Don't look for loopholes to get out of doing good.

2) OPEN YOUR HANDS (Vs 16)

Now we most likely won't have to die for another but we will most likely be inconvenienced. *(a friend needs a ride, neighbor need help fixing a lawnmower, church needs help cleaning it up, or help teaching a Bible study, or visiting the sick. You will have to share Yourself, your Resources, your Time, your Talents, wherever you have the opportunity.)*

3) OPEN YOUR HEART

John said, "Lay down your life for your brother...If anyone sees his brother in need." We are family. We must be willing to open our hearts to one another. You can not make a difference unless you open your heart not only to each other but first to God. You first have to receive His Love in the fullness before you can give it away.

Before we can actually Open Our Eyes the way God wants us to; before we can actually Open Our Hands the way God wants us to; we need to **Open Our Hearts to God. This allow Him to do whatever He needs to do to Heal Our Past** so that **He can Fill Us With His Love**, so that **He can Open Our Eyes**, so that **He can Open Our Hands**, so that **We can Love Others** the way **God has called us to.** *A type of Love that Will Make A Difference in Our World.*

To Review the 3 Points:

1) **OPEN YOUR EYES**
2) **OPEN YOUR HANDS**
3) **OPEN YOUR HEART**

(Plan of Salvation)

Admit that you have done wrong, that you can't make it to heaven without God's help. The Bible tells us that we all have sinned.

Believe that God Loves You and sent His Son Jesus to take the penalty for your sin.

Accept God's free gift of eternal life in Jesus Christ. Accept God's forgiveness and Love. Ask God to send His Holy Spirit to live in you today.

Confess Jesus as Lord and believe God raised Him from the dead and you will be saved.

Talk to God right now. He loves you and He wants you to become His child. He will listen to you. He will keep His promise to save you when you seek Him with all of your heart. He has a plan for your life. He wants to live in and through you to carry out His Will. Will you surrender to Him today? Just say, "Yes, Jesus, I surrender my will to Your Will today. I want to be born again. I want to enter into Your Kingdom. Come take complete control of my life. You come and live in me today. I don't want religion; I want a personal relationship with you. I want you Lord. I accept You not only as my Savior but also as my Lord. Make me

a new creation. Send Your Holy Spirit to live in my life from this day forward. Do Your work in and through me."
In Jesus' Name, Amen.

(see Romans 3:23, 6:23, Romans 5:8, John 3:16-18, Romans 10:9, and John 1:12)

YOU CAN MAKE A DIFFERENCE IN OUR WORLD TODAY BY LEARNING TO WALK THE TALK!

HOW TO MAKE A DIFFERENCE:

SHARE YOUR FAITH

(Acts 8:26-40 NIV) "Now an angel of the Lord said to Philip, "Go south to the road—the desert road—that goes down from Jerusalem to Gaza." So he started out, and on his way he met an Ethiopian eunuch, an important official in charge of all the treasury of the Kandake (which means "queen of the Ethiopians"). This man had gone to Jerusalem to worship, and on his way home was sitting in his chariot reading the Book of Isaiah the prophet. The Spirit told Philip, "Go to that chariot and stay near it."

Then Philip ran up to the chariot and heard the man reading Isaiah the prophet. "Do you understand what you are reading?" Philip asked.

"How can I," he said, "unless someone explains it to me?" So he invited Philip to come up and sit with him. This is the passage of Scripture the eunuch was reading:

"He was led like a sheep to the slaughter, and as a lamb before its shearer is silent, so he did not open his mouth. In his humiliation he was deprived of justice. Who can speak of his descendants? For his life was taken from the earth."

The eunuch asked Philip, "Tell me, please, who is the prophet talking about, himself or someone else?" Then Philip began with that very passage of Scripture and told him the good news about Jesus.

As they traveled along the road, they came to some water and the eunuch said, "Look, here is water. What can stand in the way of my being baptized?" And he gave orders to stop the chariot. Then both Philip and the eunuch went down into the water and Philip baptized him. When they came up out of the water, the Spirit of the Lord suddenly took Philip away, and the eunuch did not see him again, but went on his way rejoicing. Philip, however, appeared at Azotus and traveled about, preaching the gospel in all the towns until he reached Caesarea."

Today we are going to look at another way the early church made a difference. They **"Shared Their Faith"**.

Even though Sharing Your Faith is one of the most important parts of making a difference, we have to be careful of the way we share it. The messages on making a difference are important to get right in our life so that when we share our faith we will have the greatest impact. We have to live a life of "Forgiving", of "Walking the Talk", and of "Living a Live Full of God's Love" in order to share our faith most effectively.

If they can't see our Faith in Action, they won't be attracted to it. If we try to force our faith on others we may turn them off and keep them from ever being open to the Gospel.

We are going to look at three principles about witnessing that we can learn from this passage of scripture that made a difference.

1) BE SENSITIVE TO THE LEADING OF THE SPIRIT (Vs 26, 27, 29, 30)

26 "Now an angel of the Lord said to Philip, "Go..."

27 "So he started out..."

28 "The Spirit told Philip. Go..."

30 "Then Philip ran up to the chariot..."

We too, if we are sensitive to the leading to the Holy Spirit, He will lead us to people or people to us who are ready to hear our message. Sometimes we are to *plow the soil* to prepare it for receiving the seed. Sometimes we are to *plant the seed*. Sometimes we are to *fertilize and water the plant*. And sometimes we are to *Harvest the fruit*.

We need to be *sensitive* to the Holy Spirit's leading and guidance to know what needs to be done and how to do it the best. Philip was led to the Ethiopian at the right time. Philip asked him a simple non-threatening question. *"Do you understand what you are reading?"* Then he listens to see where the Ethiopian was. Sharing your faith is just that, "sharing". Not pushing or forcing. It is not doing all the talking. It involves communication between two people.

It was not a memorized sales pitch. We need to know the Word and verses and/or where to or how to find them, but we must be willing to flow with the Holy Spirit's leading.

2) TELL THEM ALL ABOUT JESUS (Vs 35)

35 "Then Philip began with that very passage of Scripture and told him the good news about Jesus."

At some time in our communication we will have to tell them about Jesus. Jesus is the person we have to get to. Not just family values, not just rights and wrongs, not just social issues, not just that there is a God out there somewhere. We have to point them to Jesus and the Cross. That is the Gospel of Jesus Christ.

(John 3:16 NIV) "For God so loved the world that he gave his one and only Son, that whoever believes in him shall not perish but have eternal life."

The only way to make a difference that lasts forever is to help people make a life-changing connection with Christ. That is our mission.

3) GIVE THEM A CHANCE TO RESPOND (Vs 36-37)

36 "As they traveled along the road, they came to some water and the eunuch said, "Look, here is water. Why shouldn't I be baptized?"

37 "Philip said, "If you believe with all your heart, you may." The eunuch answered, "I believe that Jesus Christ is the Son of God."

Philip let the Ethiopian make a decision. He didn't push him. He wanted to make sure he knew what he was doing. It has to be their decision. He qualified him with a question.

We have got a story to tell today that will make a difference. But we have to tell it in order to make a difference. They not only need to hear it, they need to see it. We need to be a giver, walking the talk, and full of God's Love sharing our faith.

(Plan of Salvation)

Admit that you have done wrong, that you can't make it to heaven without God's help. The Bible tells us that we all have sinned.

Believe that God Loves You and sent His Son Jesus to take the penalty for your sin.

Accept God's free gift of eternal life in Jesus Christ. Accept God's forgiveness and Love. Ask God to send His Holy Spirit to live in you today.

Confess Jesus as Lord and believe God raised Him from the dead and you will be saved.

Talk to God right now. He loves you and He wants you to become His child. He will listen to you. He will keep His promise to save you when you seek Him with all of your heart. He has a plan for your life. He wants to live in and through you to carry out His Will. Will you surrender to Him today?

Just say, **"Yes, Jesus, I surrender my will to Your Will today. I want to be born again. I want to enter into Your Kingdom. Come take complete control of my life. You come and live in me today. I don't want religion; I want a personal relationship with you. I want you Lord. I accept You not only as my Savior but also as my Lord. Make me a new creation. Send Your Holy Spirit to live in my life from this day forward. Do Your work in and through me."**
In Jesus' Name, Amen.

(see Romans 3:23, 6:23, Romans 5:8, John 3:16-18, Romans 10:9, and John 1:12)

YOU CAN MAKE A DIFFERENCE IN OUR WORLD TODAY BY SHARING YOUR FAITH!

A MOTHER'S FAITH MAKES A DIFFERENCE

(2 Timothy 1:5-6 NIV)

"I am reminded of your sincere faith, which first lived in your grandmother Lois and in your mother Eunice and, I am persuaded, now lives in you also. For this reason I remind you to fan into flame the gift of God, which is in you through the laying on of my hands."

In the mid-1900's, an editor of a London newspaper wanted to write an article on the importance of teachers and chose to inquire with Winston Churchill, Prime Minister of England, to find out which of his teachers he attributed his success. He was unable to get a personal interview with Winston Churchill so he sent him a questionnaire to answer. He researched all the known teachers and political figures that Winston Churchill had worked or studied under and included all of these in this questionnaire. Then he wrote a letter saying, "Sir, would you please complete this survey? I would like to run a story in the paper about the great influence teachers have upon our lives."

After a few weeks the editor received the questionnaire back completely blank, except for one comment at the bottom of the page. Churchill had written, "You have omitted to mention the greatest of my teachers - **my mother**!"

Even though this today is geared towards mothers, we can all apply these six (6) principles to make a difference to those whom we have influence with.

1) PRINCIPLES -Teach your children the principles of God.

They need to be taught the principles of unconditional love, forgiveness, mercy, and grace. They need to know that they can bring anything to God in prayer and that faith in God is always the best choice. They need to see God as one that loves them no matter what mistakes they may make. He is always wanting and waiting to forgive you and help you to be that special person He created you to be.

2) PATTERN- Set a pattern in your life that reflects the life of Jesus.

Children learn by watching what you do and seeing how you handle things, more than by how you tell them to be. How do you live your life? Can your children see Jesus when they watch you day to day? If you make a mistake do you omit it quickly and ask forgiveness to those involved and to God. Do you demonstrate humbleness? They will learn so much by that humble attitude.

What kind of jokes do you tell? What do you watch on TV? Ask yourself a question, "If Jesus was here today, Would He be doing what I am doing?" If not you may want to change your pattern.

3) PERSISTENT- Be persistent in your faith.

Teach your children the difference between right and wrong. Not from a worldly point of view because that changes daily, but for the Word of God. Let them know that the Bible is the Standard to Stand on Always. If the Bible calls it Sin, It is Sin. When you make your decision based on the Word of God then you can Stand Strong because no matter what His Word will always be right. Let your children see that no matter what you can persistently go to God and His Word for the Truth and you strive to persistently follow His Word in all you do.

4) PARTICIPATE- Participate in your child's life.

Become your Child's Best Friend. Take time to spend with them. Find out what is important to them. Really get to know them. God wants us to know that He is our Best Friend, and the same is true of you and your children. They need to know that you are on their side.

5) PRAISE-Praise your children for the good things they do.

It has been found that so many people are so starved for attention that if they don't get praise for doing good things, they will often do the wrong things just to get attention. If we don't give them praise for the good they will do negative just to get attention. Look for ways to Praise them.

6) PRAY- Pray for and with your children.

The memory of a Mom or Dad interceding for you in prayer will never escape your mind. The times you kneel beside the bed, place your hand on them and prayed with and for them will always be there in their memory.

REVIEW:

Paul knew that if Timothy would just think back and remember the faith of his mother and grandmother, **he would remember**:

1. The PRINCIPLES of God.
2. To PATTERN his life after Jesus Christ.
3. To be PERSISTENT in his faith.
4. To PARTICIPATE in the life of others. Become their best friend and they will remember.
5. To give PRAISE whenever possible.
6. To PRAY, PRAY, PRAY, for and with them.

What type of faith are you passing down to your children, grand children, or those that look up to you for guidance?

Does it reflect God's love, forgiveness, mercy and understanding?

Today, no matter the past, I challenge each of us to start where we are and apply these principles. They will make a difference in the lives of those we have influence over.

A MOTHER'S FAITH MAKES A DIFFERENCE

Ledora (Betty) McDonald (Picture 1974)

Nanny Broome (1968) *Nanny Chandler (1951)*

(2 Timothy 1:5-6 My Version) *"I am reminded of your sincere faith, which first lived in your grandmothers Nanny Broome and Nanny Chandler and in your mother Ledora (Betty) McDonald and, I am persuaded, now lives in you also. For this reason I remind you to fan into flame the gift of God, which is in you through the laying on of my hands."*

I Love You and Thank You All!

The Seed and The Soil

Mark 4:3-8, 13-20

"Listen! A farmer went out to sow his seed. As he was scattering the seed, some fell along the path, and the birds came and ate it up. Some fell on rocky places, where it did not have much soil. It sprang up quickly, because the soil was shallow. But when the sun came up, the plants were scorched, and they withered because they had no root. Other seed fell among thorns, which grew up and choked the plants, so that they did not bear grain. Still other seed fell on good soil. It came up, grew and produced a crop, some multiplying thirty, some sixty, some a hundred times."

"...Then Jesus said to them, "Don't you understand this parable? How then will you understand any parable? The farmer sows the word. Some people are like seed along the path, where the word is sown. As *soon as they hear it, Satan comes and takes away the word that was sown in them. Others, like seed sown on rocky places, hear the word and at once receive it with joy. But since they have no root, they last only a short time. When trouble or persecution comes because of the word, they quickly fall away. Still others, like seed sown among thorns, hear the word; but the worries of this life, the deceitfulness of wealth and the desires for other things come in and choke the word, making it unfruitful. Others, like seed sown on good soil, hear the word, accept it, and produce a crop—some thirty, some sixty, some a hundred times what was sown."*

Here we have what is known as the *"Parable of the Sower"*. But as we look at this perhaps we should call it the *"Parable of the Soils"*. Because Jesus is telling us more about 4 types of Soils or 4 types of People then the seed or the sower. Everyone here today is like one of these types of Soils. Some may even be like a combination of two.

And "The Seed" is the Word of God.

1) **Verse 15** says, *"Some people are like seed along the path, where the word is sown. As soon as they hear it, Satan comes and takes away the word that was sown* *in them."* The <u>hardened path</u> represents those with a <u>Hardened Heart</u>. They hear the Gospel but will not accept it. Often they will even turn and go the opposite way because their Heart is hardened. Their minds are closed to anything about the Gospel.

2) Verse 16 & 17 says, *"Others, like seed sown on rocky places, hear the word and at once receive it with joy. But since they have no root, they last only a short time. When trouble or persecution comes because of the word, they quickly fall away."* The <u>Rocky Soil</u> represents those that have a <u>Stony Heart.</u> They are <u>not</u> hardened like the first ones. When they hear the Gospel they receive it gladly. But the trouble is they have no root. They only last for a short time. They may look Christian for a short time but soon they will start looking more like the World than like Jesus. They don't really get into the word and obey it.

This is one reason why Paul stated in **1 Timothy 3:6** that a <u>Deacon</u> or an <u>Overseer</u> ***"must <u>not</u> be a recent convert, or he may become conceited and fall under the same judgment as the devil."*** Paul is telling Timothy to be sure that they have deep roots that will soak up the water and nutrients of God's Word and obey them not just for a short time but their lives will become one of obedience to Jesus.

3) Verse 18 &19 says, *"Still others, like seed sown among thorns, hear the word; but the worries of this life, the deceitfulness of wealth and the desires for other things come in and choke the word, making it unfruitful."*

These people also receive the Gospel and start off like the one before it. They started looking like a Christian but it does not last either. This type of soil is Cluttered Soil with *briers* and *thorns*. They represent the Cluttered Life that allows worries and materialism come in and choke the word and prevents the maturing of Fruit. These are those that will not put God's Will first. These are those will not surrender and Do What Jesus Would Do. *Often because they believe that they would not make as much money if they did what Jesus would do. Or that they would not have as much fun if they Did What Jesus Would Do.*

My question to them is *"Are you really saved or has Satan come and fooled you into believing that you are saved but you don't need to really live a pure life?"* You need to read **John 15** again. We must remain in the Vine or we will be cut off and thrown into the fire and burned. God's will is to have us bear much fruit. *If you are not doing what Jesus would do then you are not* *producing the Fruit of Jesus.* <u>You may not even be saved because Satan has killed the life of the Word that was once alive in you and you may not even know it.</u> In **Matt.7** Jesus says <u>only</u> those that does the will of the Father will enter the kingdom of heaven.

4) Verse 20 says, ***"Others, like seed sown on good soil, hear the word, accept it, and produce a crop thirty, sixty, or even a hundred times what was sown."*** These are the only ones that I am sure, are saved. This is the kind of soil I want to be. I hope You desire to be the Good Soil also.

No Matter what Soil you are now, you can be made Good Soil by surrender to the sower, God. God wants to plow up your life, get the rocks out, get the weeds out, fertilize you with the Word, water you with the Holy Spirit so you will produce His Fruit. 30, 60, and 100 times what was sown.

PREPARING FOR REVIVAL

2 Chronicles 7:14 NIV

"If my people, who are called by my name, will humble themselves and pray and seek my face and turn from their wicked ways, then will I hear from heaven and will forgive their sin and will heal their land."

Our week of Special Services is only four weeks away now. How can we be preparing for them? How can we prepare for Revival? Not only by getting the word out about these meetings but how do we prepare personally?

I think we can see four elements for revival in 2 Chronicles 7:14. The four elements are: 1) Relationship- 2) Repentance- 3) Restoration- 4) Regeneration-

1) <u>Relationship</u> - *"If my people, who are called by my name, will humble themselves and pray and seek my face and turn from their wicked ways..."*

    Revival starts with God's People. Every Revival in History started with God's People humbling themselves and praying and seeking God's face and turning from their wicked ways. Revival starts when we humble ourselves, pray, seek His face, and turn from our wicked ways.

2) <u>Repentance</u>- *"If my people, who are called by my name, will humble themselves and pray and seek my face and turn from their wicked ways, then will I hear from heaven ..."*

Repentance involves Confessing Sin. There will be no revival until we confess our sins, turn from our evil ways, and throw ourselves upon God's mercy.

Psalm 66:18 says: *"If I regard iniquity in my heart, the Lord will not hear me."*

Any and all things that will slow down or reroute the flow of God's grace must be removed. What kind of sin?

Sin like: unbelief, lust, lying, cheating, unclean thoughts, filthy talk, , dirty habits, cursing, gossiping, not being thankful, disregard of self discipline, lack of prayer, robbing God of His tithes, neglecting the poor, racial discrimination, an unforgiving spirit, backbiting, envy, jealousy, bitterness, deceitfulness, selfishness, etc.

Whatever it is, whether a deed or just an attitude about us, if known to be contrary to the holiness of God, it must be confessed and turned away from. No compromise. It is a time of Thorough Housecleaning.

Not only must confession be made to God; we must do all we can to make things right with the people we have wronged. And if none of the list above hit home with you then perhaps the prayer in Psalm 139:23-24 will be a good place to start. ***"Search me, O God, and know my heart: try me, and know my thoughts: And see if there be any wicked way in me...."***

The Holy Spirit will reveal them.

After we have confessed and turned away from our wicked ways we can become clean. The Bible tells us **"If we confess our sins He is faithful and just and will forgive us of our sins and purify us from all unrighteousness." 1 John 1:9 NIV**

When we become clean, the Spirit of God can flow through the believing heart in true intercessory prayer.

Revival will come when His people come together in unity and prevail in prayer.

If we look at Acts 1 and 2, we can see that they all joined together constantly in prayer. All were together in unity. All were Seeking God's Will. And God showed up.

Acts 2:2-4 NIV
"Suddenly a sound like the blowing of a violent wind came from heaven and filled the whole house where they were sitting. They saw what seemed to be tongues of fire that separated and came to rest on each of them. All of them were filled with the Holy Spirit and began to speak in other tongues as the Spirit enabled them."

Verse 41 reveals the outcome. Three Thousand were saved.

3) **Restoration** - or Renewal of the backsliders. A renewal of those that accepted Christ, but have not lived for Him.

"then will I hear from heaven and will forgive their sin ..."

A Renewal of many that have been as dead men will be renewed, revived and refreshed. They will be alive again. They will be restored and live full of the Spirit of God.

4) **Regeneration**- I *"will heal their land."* God said He will heal our land. In the healing of the land will be a great harvest.

Not only will the Christians come alive, on fire for the Lord Jesus Christ, but the lost will be drawn to the light of the fire and the renewed life of the Church and they too will be saved.

Do we really want Revival in this area? God Says: *"If my people, who are called by my name, will humble themselves and pray and seek my face and turn from their wicked ways, then will I hear from heaven and will forgive their sin and will heal their land."*

Will we do this? Will we humble ourselves and pray and seek God's face and turn from our wicked ways? If we will God says: *"then He will hear from heaven and will forgive our sin and will heal our land."*

This is what we need to do these next four weeks. We need to be sure that first that we are right with God, and then pray and intercede for our community.

Ask, God to Let His Glory Fall in this room. Ask for His Kingdom to come. Then be ready for God to move make a difference in those around us. Be ready to serve where needed as He brings in the Harvest.

The End or The Beginning of Revival?

(Given on the last night of a Community Tent Revival Meeting in Jackson, SC)

Tonight we are ending up a week of Special Services here in Jackson, South Carolina for 1997. But we don't have to end what God has started. We need to continue to seek Jesus more and prepare for the great harvest that He is planning in Jackson.

God has blessed this community with some great anointed Pastors and has placed them here for a very special purpose of changing Jackson for the Kingdom of God. And for some reason God has sent me and my family also to Jackson for this special time. I feel privileged just to be here and share with you tonight. I believe that God has brought us together for a purpose. This is His purpose.

And we need to get ready for what He is planning to do in Jackson. But the question becomes, **will we allow what He is planning or not?**

How many of you know that God has been moving all over the world in a mighty way?

I don't know if you knew it but since January 1994, God has been pouring out His Spirit in a mighty Renewal at the Toronto Airport Christian Fellowship in Canada. They have been in a renewal that has brought in hundreds of thousands of Christians from all over the world to that church to be renewed and refreshed in the love and power of God. Many pastors and leaders that were dry and ready to give up are now alive and on fire for God like never before. Many of the people that have went to Canada have caught some of that renewing and refreshing and brought it back to where they came from and have been able to spread it to others that are hungry for more of God.

In Pensacola Florida at Brownsville Assembly of God on Father's Day 1995, God showed up mightily. Since then they have been in a mighty outpouring of the Holy Spirit. A mighty Revival has been going on. Not only have God's People gotten right with Him but over 100,000 salvations have taken place there in just over two years. People from all over the world are being drawn to that church and their lives are being changed. Many of the people that went there have caught some of the revival fire and have been able to take it back to their area and start a revival fire there also.

Not only has God blessed my wife and me by moving us to Jackson this past year. He has also blessed us by letting us go to and experience part of what is going on at Toronto and Pensacola. I know that God did not just send us there just to be doing it. I know that God has brought this group of Pastors to Jackson not just to be doing it. I know that God has brought these churches together this week not just to be doing it. God has planned this for a purpose. You are here tonight for a purpose. And if you will be open to the Lord tonight, and respond to His Holy Spirit, He can and will change your life. He will renew, refresh and revive you so that you can and will make a difference in the Jackson area and because of that change there will be a great harvest of souls in the whole area. Jackson will be different.

So to start off I want everyone to repeat after me, out loud, a simple prayer.

Dear LORD,
> Speak to my heart, Change my life.
>> In Your Precious Name.

If you have your Bibles turn to 2 Chronicles 7:14. I am sure you have heard this verse before, but it is so important that I believe we will visit it again.

***(2 Chronicles 7:14 NIV)** "If my people, who are called by my name, will humble themselves and pray and seek my face and turn from their wicked ways, then will I hear from heaven and will forgive their sin and will heal their land."*

Within this one verse are several keys to renewal, refreshing, revival and a great harvest.

Tonight I want to look at this verse and try to take 4 key points here and apply them to help unlock us to a life of renewal, refreshing and revival that will make a difference not only in our own lives, but also in our families, our churches and our community. If we apply these we can see all of Jackson brought into the Kingdom of God.

<u>**Key 1**</u> - *"If my people, who are called by my name,..."*

God is talking to His People that are called by His Name.

Revival starts with God's People. Every Revival in History started with God's People. Revival starts when we, those that are called by His Name, wake up and start doing what He has called us to do. This verse is talking about me and you.

Key 2 - *"If my people, who are called by my name, will humble themselves and pray and seek my face and turn from their wicked ways, then will I hear from heaven ..."*

We need to Repent! I said we need to repent, and I am including myself. Repentance involves Confessing Sin. To repent means to turn from. No revival will come until we confess our sin, turn from our evil ways, and throw ourselves upon God's mercy.

Psalm 66:18 says*:* *"If I regard <u>iniquity</u> in my heart, the Lord will not hear me."*

In the Webster Dictionary *<u>iniquity</u>* is defined as: *a wicked, unjust, or unrighteous act.*

Any and all things that will slow down or reroute the flow of God's grace to and through us must be removed. What kind of sin? Not just the ones that we often think of as big sins. Any sin to God is wicked no matter how small we think it is.

See, God is a Holy God and He wants us to be Holy too. He tells us that in 1 Peter 1:16. We need to repent of any sin no matter how small we may think it is. I am not only talking about the sins that others can see but the <u>secret hidden sins</u> that we have been keeping in our closets. Those sins that we think are hid and only we and God know about. Sins like:

<u>lust, pornography</u>, (TV and Magazines, do we turn from them or do we find ourselves looking even though we know it is not right. Maybe we are all by ourselves, but God sees you.)

<u>lying</u>, <u>cheating</u>, (I once heard someone that was supposed to be a leader at his church openly lie to someone on the phone and afterward say, "I can lie pretty good can't I?" as if he was proud of it.)

<u>unclean thoughts</u>, (What do we think about that we do not want to tell about in church on Sunday morning? God knows our thoughts.)

unpure talk, filthy speech, dirty habits, cursing, (What kind of jokes or gestures do we either do or participate in?)

gossiping, (Do we only say things that will lift someone up or are we saying things that will hurt them? I know my mother used to tell me, "If you can't say anything good about someone, then don't say anything!")

not being thankful, (Did you know that not being thankful is a sin. We are blessed so much in the United States, but we take most of it for granted.)

racial discrimination, (We still don't realize that there is only one Race. It is the Human Race and Jesus died for that Race.) God has called us to love each other. Jesus loved us all so much that He suffered and died on the cross for each person, no matter what the color of our skin is. He tells us to love one another as He has loved us.

In **1 John 4:20** the Word of God says, *"If anyone say, "I love God," yet hates his brother, he is a liar. For anyone who does no love his brother, whom he has seen, cannot love God, whom he has not seen."*

unforgivness, (There are some around Jackson that have still not forgiven the Plant from coming and taking away their land and their way of life before Savannah River Site. They hold it against those that even work there today. There are some that have unforgivness for past ministers, church members, and neighbors. Unforgivness is a Sin and we must forgive others.)

pride, (That is a bigger one that most of us think. Pride we tell you not to go forward at the altar call. I know that Pride kept me from going forward just a few weeks ago when I knew God was calling me to go forward in a service I was in. I would try to reason with God, "God I know that you can hear me here in my seat and that I really don't have to go forward to get right with you, after all I am a Pastor, and what will the people think?" Have you ever done that? That is the sin of Pride. And Pride will keep us from being totally set free. **"If my people, who are called by my name, will humble themselves** ... Remember Jesus died publicly for you, will you come publicly to him?

I could go on and on....

Whatever it is, whether a deed or just an attitude about us, if known to be contrary to the holiness of God, it must be confessed and turned away from. No compromise.

It is a time for thorough Housecleaning. Not only must confession be made to God; we must do all we can to make things right with the people we have wronged.

Matthew 5:23-24 say, *"If you are offering your gift at the altar and there remember that your brother has something against you, leave your gift there in front of the altar, First go and be reconciled to you brother; then come and offer your gift."*

And if none of the list above hits home with you, then perhaps the prayer in **Psalm 139:23-24** will be a good place to start. It says,

"Search me, O God, and know my heart: try me, and know my thoughts: And see if there be any wicked way in me...."

The Holy Spirit will reveal them to you.

We need to become clean vessel, so that the Spirit of God can flow through us to make a difference in the Jackson area. I can think of an example here in Jackson by knowing what we on the Fire Department often will have to do. Sometimes a drainage pipe under the street will get clogged up with trash and debris and the town will use the Fire Department to use the Fire Engine and high pressure hose lines to flush and clean out the pipes with water so that the storm water will flow freely. Interesting also is that often "water" is a picture of the Holy Spirit and we too need some flushing of our lives to remove the trash and debris we have allowed to build up inside of us.

Key 3- The **Renewal of the backsliders**. And I believe that most of us have either been one at one time or might even be one now. We need a renewal of those that accepted Christ at one time, but have not lived completely for Him.

God says, **"If my people, who are called by my name, will humble themselves and pray and seek my face and turn from their wicked ways, then will I hear from heaven and will forgive their sin ..."**

The indication here is that without humbling ourselves, praying, seeking God and turning from our sins, He will not hear us.

Remember the story Jesus told of the two men that went up to the temple to pray in **Luke 18.** *One was a Pharisee and the other a tax collector. The Pharisee* *stood up and prayed about himself. He said, "God I thank you that I am not like other men - robbers, evildoers, adulterers - or even like this tax collector. I fast twice a week and give a tenth of all I get."*

"But the tax collector stood at a distance. He would not even look up to heaven, but beat his breast and said, "God, Have mercy on me, a sinner."

Remember what Jesus said? He tells us that it was the tax collector that went home justified before God, not the Pharisee which was the religious leader of that day.

<u>After we have confessed and turned away from our wicked ways we will become clean.</u> The Bible tells us *"If we confess our sins He is faithful and just and will forgive us of our sins and purify us from all unrighteousness." 1 John 1:9*

As we return back to love God with all of our heart, soul, mind and strength we will renewed, revived and refreshed. We will become alive again. We will be restored and alive with a fullness of the Spirit that most only read about in the Bible.

The Church of Jesus Christ needs this today. The Church in Jackson needs this today. We personally need this today. We all need to be Renewed. We all need more of God's Love and Power in our lives today.

I believe that one reason why many will not come to Jesus today is because when they look at the Church, they don't see Jesus. When they look at us they don't see Jesus in us. They don't see Jesus in me and in you. They don't see us doing and living how the Bible tells us the early followers of Jesus did.

The Church is called the "Body of Christ". We need to start being the "Body of Christ", not only in word, but with action and deeds by the power and guidance of the Holy Spirit.

Then and only then will we see.... Key number 4.

Key 4- I *"If my people, who are called by my name, will humble themselves and pray and seek my face and turn from their wicked ways, then will I hear from heaven and will forgive their sin <u>will heal their land."</u>*

God said He will heal our land. In the healing of the land there will be a <u>Great Harvest</u> of Souls. Not only will the Christians come alive and be on fire for the Lord Jesus Christ, but the lost will be drawn to the light of the fire like a bug is drawn to a light when it is dark outside. Once they are drawn and see the real Light of the World, <u>they too will be saved</u>. Because the Bible tells us when *<u>Jesus Christ is lifted up He will draw all men to Him</u>*. John 12:32

When we do the above and become what God is calling us to be, people that are just driving through Jackson going to the beach or to work will come under the conviction of the Holy Spirit and will be drawn to Jesus Christ. They will feel the difference. There will be a different atmosphere around Jackson. There will be a fragrance in the air that will make people hungry for God. Just like when one drive through New Ellenton and the smell the smoke of Carolina Bar-B-Que. Just the smell makes you hungry for barbecue when you drive through New Ellenton. You been there and you know that your mouth starts watering as you smell the smoke. People will also notice the difference around here as they pass through and become hungry for God.

Do we really want a Renewal, a Refreshing, a Revival and a Great Harvest of Souls in Jackson?

God Says: *"If my people, who are called by my name, will humble themselves and pray and seek my face and turn from their wicked ways, then will I hear from heaven and will forgive their sin and will heal their land."*

Will we do this? Will we humble ourselves and pray and seek God's face and turn from <u>all</u> our wicked ways?

If we will do that, God says: **"then He will hear from heaven and will forgive our sin and will heal our land."**

On the first night of these meetings, Pastor Allen Cantrell said it and it is still the message tonight.

"When God's People get right, Lost People get saved!"

It is all up to each of us tonight. If this week is to make a difference, it is up to us. If we will get right with God, then we will be different and become more like Jesus, the lost will see the difference and be drawn to Jesus and they will be saved and we will see Jackson won for Jesus.

I want all pastors to come forward now to not only set the example but to be ready for what God is going to do.

I want to open up the altar now and I want everyone to respond. I'll say it again, <u>I want everyone to respond</u>. No matter whom you are. No matter what your relationship to God is tonight. We all have sinned we all have made mistakes, myself included, and we all need more of God's Love and His Power working in and through us in order to make a real difference in Jackson.

Not only do I want you to come forward tonight, but I know that God is waiting and longing for you to come to Him right now.

If you have never asked Jesus to come into your life, you come.

<u>You may not have another chance</u>. You may not even live to see tomorrow. I know that, As a Paramedic I have seen lots of people die, young and old. Many if not most were not expecting that it was their last day. But it was.

If there is any unconfessed sin in your life, even the so called secret hidden sins. You come.

If you have been saved but you have backslidden and you are not as close to God as you know you should be, you come.

If you are just hungry and thirsty for more of God's Holy Spirit working in and through you, come.

You may have an illness or sickness that you need God to help you through or heal you from; you come.

No matter what your need is or who you are, I am asking you to come to the altar and receive from God tonight.

Yes, *God can hear you where you are and touch you where you are*, but if that is what you are saying to yourself right now, that's **"Pride"**. <u>If Pride is one of the sins that is keeping you from coming forward you better step out and come right now</u>. <u>Don't be like I was</u>. Don't put off getting completely right with God. God does not want to play games anymore. <u>He is getting His Church ready for the next mighty move of His Holy Spirit and He wants all of His Church to be ready</u>. So you come. You Come Tonight. Come.

HOW TO ENJOY THE WINNING LIFE

(Deuteronomy 28:13 NIV)

"The Lord will make you the head, not the tail. If you pay attention to the commands of the Lord your God that I give you this day and carefully follow them, you will always be at the top, never at the bottom."

Everyone wants to have a winning life. The strong desire to experience personal fulfillment and to able to reach their full potential, is built into every human being.

(Ephesians 2:10 NIV)
"For We are God's workmanship, created In Christ Jesus to do good works, which God prepared in advance for us to do."

We need to reach out for the greatness that God has planned for each of us. He is the Master Designer and has

Created us to do good works. God has designed each of us to be a success. God has a purpose for each one. God doesn't create any failures. Each person is a special creation of God.

Each of us is unique, what makes you feel successful may not be what makes another person feel successful. God planned it that way. God also sometimes changes our direction from what was our calling and made us feel successful at one season in our life to another direction and calling. It all is in His Hands and His Timing. We just have to continue to surrender to Him and seek His Will. Each one of us is different and special. Each one of us has an important part to play in life. Each one of us has an important part to play in God's plan. No matter how that plan evolves within God's overall plan, we are designed to be winners in Christ. We are to have Victory in Jesus to reach our full potential in Christ.

A winning life has been defined as a consistent and progressive achievement of worth while, God intended goals for your life.

God created you to achieve certain goals and He gave you the talents and abilities to reach them.

Here are **five essential ingredients** that will help you live a worthwhile and meaningful life. Here are **five essential ingredients that will let you enjoy the winning life** and to help you reach your full potential in Christ.

1) MAKE THE EFFORT TO RECONSTRUCT THE CORRECT CONCEPT OF GOD.

A) DISCARD THE WRONG "GOD-PICTURE".

How do you see God? If you picture God as a harsh dictator or far-distant Higher Power, you have not seen God in the correct light.

Jesus called Him, *"Father."* Jesus not only called Him *"Father",* He described Him as a forgiving, loving, caring, restoring, and blessing Father. Remember the Parable of the Prodigal Son and the Loving, Forgiving Father. **(Luke 15:11-32)**

B) DEVELOP THE TRUE "GOD-PICTURE".

If we want to really see God the Father we can just look at Jesus. Just put our eyes on Jesus. Jesus said... ***"he that has seen me has seen the Father."*** **(John 14:9)** Jesus also said that he only did the things that pleased the Father. **(John 8:28, 29)**

What were the works Jesus did? He healed the sick, fed the hungry, comforted those that troubled and gave hope to the hopeless.

This is what God is like: **"For God so loved the world that He gave His one and only Son so that whoever believes, in Him shall not perish but have eternal life."** (John 3:16)

Take time to read your Bible this week and see how good and kind your Heavenly Father is! He cares about you and wants you to have a winning life.

2) RECOGNIZE THE LIMITATIONS OF SATAN.

"Submit yourselves, then to God. Resist the devil, and he will flee from you." **(James 4:7)**

One of the **definitions of "Submit" is "Surrender"**. Anyone who is in Christ and submitted to, or surrendered to God has nothing to fear from Satan. The Bible says... *"greater is He that is in you than he that is in the world."* **(1 John 4:4)**

The Bible says, *"And God raised us up with Christ and seated us with Him in the heavenly realms in Christ Jesus."* **(Ephesians 2:6)** *"And God place all things under His feet"* **(Ephesians 1:22).** This all things include Satan. So today Satan is under your feet when you are in Christ. **Romans 8:37** declares... *"we are more than conquerors through Him who loved us."*

Remember Satan is limited, but the power of God is unlimited!

3. REACH OUT TO THOSE WHO ARE HURTING AROUND YOU.

(Philippians 2:4) *"Each of you should look not only to your own interest, but also to the interests of others."*

(1 Corinthians 10:24) *"Nobody should seek his own good, but the good of others."*

One of the most vital lessons you will ever learn is the importance of other people to your life. To have a winning life, you must need to concentrate on helping others succeed. (**1 Kings 17**: The widow woman first fed **Elijah**, and then the Lord fed her).

Jesus loved people and, moved by His compassion, went about doing good. The Bible says, *"Whoever claims to live in Him must walk as Jesus did."* (1 John 2:6)

Winners are people who cultivate a loving, caring attitude toward others. **Galatians 6:2** says, *"Carry each other's burdens, and in this way you will fulfill the law of Christ."* Galatians 6:10 says, *..."as we have opportunity, let us do good to all people, especially to those who belong to the family of believers."* Let us concentrate on helping someone else to win today.

4) RESPECT YOURSELF AS A VALUABLE CREATION OF AN ALMIGHTY GOD.

1 Peter 2:9 *"But you are a chosen people, a royal priesthood, a holy nation, a people belonging to God, that you may declare the praises of him who call you out of darkness into his wonderful light."*

A) STOP SEEING YOURSELF AS OTHERS SEE YOU.

You must build a good picture of yourself to enjoy the winning life. Most people will point out all of your weaknesses, rather than your strengths. This negative conditioning makes us failure-conscious, so that we become *"problem-oriented"* rather that *"possibility-oriented"*.

1) **Moses** gave God all the reasons why he was unfit for the great work God called him to, but God gave him solutions for every problem.

2) **Gideon,** too, said he was not good enough for the job God wanted him to do. But God saw him as a *"mighty warrior."* God saw the possibility in Gideon and what God was going to do through him. You can read that God did use Gideon, but first Gideon had to see himself as God did before he became transformed into that mighty warrior. **(Judges 6)**

3) **Paul** declared in **Philippians 4:13**, *"I can do all things through Christ who give me strength."*

B) START SEEING YOURSELF AS GOD SEES YOU.

1) **"Therefore if any man be in Christ, he is a new creature: old things are passed away; behold, all things are become new." (2 Corinthians 5:17)**

2) *"There is therefore now no condemnation to them which are in Christ Jesus, who walk not after the flesh, but after the Spirit."* (Romans 8:1)

3) *"And be not conformed to the world: but be ye transformed by the renewing of your mind...."* (Romans 12:2)

4) *" ... Ye have put off the old man with his deeds; and have put on the new man, which is renewed in knowledge after the image of Him that created him."* (Colossians 3:9, 10)

5) SURRENDER TO GOD SO THAT HE CAN WORK IN AND THROUGH YOU.

A) ONLY HE KNOWS YOUR FULL POTENTIAL

B) ONLY THROUGH HIM CAN YOU REACH YOUR FULL POTENTIAL

Admit that you have done wrong.

Believe that God Loves You and sent His Son Jesus to take the penalty for your sin.

Accept God's free gift of eternal life in Jesus Christ.

Confess Jesus as Lord and believe God raised Him from the dead and you will be saved.

Talk to God right now. He loves you and He wants you to become His child. He will listen to you. He will keep His promise to save you when you seek Him with all of your heart. He has a plan for your life. He wants to live in and through you to carry out His Will. Will you surrender to Him today?

Just say, *"Yes, Heavenly Father, I surrender my will to Your Will today. Come take complete control of my life. You come and live in me today. I don't want religion; I want a personal relationship with you. I want you Lord."*

"The Events of the Cross"

Matthew 27:27-56 NIV

"Then the governor's soldiers took Jesus into the Praetorium and gathered the whole company of soldiers around him. They stripped him and put a scarlet robe on him, and then twisted together a crown of thorns and set it on his head. They put a staff in his right hand. Then they knelt in front of him and mocked him. "Hail, king of the Jews!" they said. They spit on him, and took the staff and struck him on the head again and again. After they had mocked him, they took off the robe and put his own clothes on him. Then they led him away to crucify him."

"As they were going out, they met a man from Cyrene, named Simon, and they forced him to carry the cross. They came to a place called Golgotha (which means "the place of the skull"). There they offered

Jesus wine to drink, mixed with gall; but after tasting it, he refused to drink it." "When they had crucified him, they divided up his clothes by casting lots. And sitting down, they kept watch over him there. Above his head they placed the written charge against him: THIS IS JESUS, THE KING OF THE JEWS."

"Two rebels were crucified with him, one on his right and one on his left. Those who passed by hurled insults at him, shaking their heads and saying, "You who are going to destroy the temple and build it in three days, save yourself! Come down from the cross, if you are the Son of God!" In the same way the chief priests, the teachers of the law and the elders mocked him. "He saved others," they said, "but he can't save himself! He's the king of Israel! Let him come down now from the cross, and we will believe in him. He trusts in God. Let God rescue him now if he wants him, for he said, 'I am the Son of God.'" In the same way the rebels who were crucified with him also heaped insults on him."

"From noon until three in the afternoon darkness came over all the land. About three in the afternoon Jesus cried out in a loud voice, "Eli, Eli, lema sabachthani?" (which means "My God, my God, why have you forsaken me?").

When some of those standing there heard this, they said, "He's calling Elijah."

"Immediately one of them ran and got a sponge. He filled it with wine vinegar, put it on a staff, and offered it to Jesus to drink. The rest said, "Now leave him alone. Let's see if Elijah comes to save him."

"And when Jesus had cried out again in a loud voice, he gave up his spirit."

"At that moment the curtain of the temple was torn in two from top to bottom. The earth shook, the rocks split and the tombs broke open. The bodies of many holy people who had died were raised to life. They came out of the tombs after Jesus' resurrection and went into the holy city and appeared to many people."

"When the centurion and those with him who were guarding Jesus saw the earthquake and all that had happened, they were terrified, and exclaimed, "Surely he was the Son of God!"

"Many women were there, watching from a distance. They had followed Jesus from Galilee to care for his needs. Among them were Mary Magdalene, Mary the mother of James and Joseph, and the mother of Zebedee's sons".

INTRODUCTION: We have just read the account of the actual crucifixion of Jesus Christ as recorded by Matthew. To see a more complete picture of all the events that took place we would have to read all four accounts of the event from Matthew, Mark, Luke and John. By reading all of them we can see the more of the events that transpired there.

Today I would like to look at several RESPONSES to the events of the cross. Many of these responses will come from these verses in Matthew. At times I will mention other scripture to refer to. Feel free to write down some of the other verses so that you can reflect on them to get more of an impact of what happen on the cross some 2000 years ago.

RESPONSES TO THE EVENTS OF THE CROSS

1) **The Response of Nature:** Vs 50-53.

The entire universe responded. After all this was no ordinary man that was crucified. This was the creator of the universe. **John 1 says, *"Through Him all things were made..."***

1. Graves were opened Vs 52
2. Darkness   Vs 45
3. The feeling of death hung over the entire earth
4. Earthquakes   Vs 54

2) **The Response of Humanity:** Vs 36 ..."*sitting down they kept watch over Him there.*"

We can see that people that were watching Him were in two different groups. They were either non-believers or believers. Let us see how they responded to the event that took place on the cross in different ways.

In verses 39-44 we see:
1. Unbelief -
2. Mocking Him -
3. Rejection -

But in verses 54-56 we see others that believed in Jesus.
1. The centurion - Vs 54
2. Many women - Vs 55
3. Close friends and relatives - 56

3) **The Response of the Father:** Vs 46 Jesus said, *"My God, my God, why have You forsaken me?"*

Now one of the first questions I would have is what does that mean? I believe that there were two things that this verse shows us.

<u>1</u>. Jesus was still trying to witness to those around Him then and to us today who He was and what was going on. Remember at that time the Bible did not have chapter and verses as we have today. This came several hundred years at a latter time. If someone wanted to relate to a part of the Word they would often quote the first part of it so that others would know what part they were relating to. Here Jesus quotes the Psalm 22:1 and in Psalm 22 we can see much of what was taken place. Parts of **Psalm 22** says *..."all my bones are out of joint",* and *..."They have pierced my hands and my feet"* and *..."They divide my garments among they and cast lots for my clothing".* Jesus could have been trying to tell the ones that are doing this to Him to look and see that He was the one told about in the Old Testament.

<u>2</u>. But more importantly I believe God the Father was show His Great Love for Us. What was taking place was really more that we could see in the physical. God did turn His back on Jesus as Jesus took on our sins.

2 Corinthians 5:21 says, *"God made Him who had no sin to be sin for us, so that in Him we might become the righteousness of God."*

John 3:16 says, *"For God so loved the world that He gave His one and only Son, that whoever believes in Him shall not perish but have eternal life."*

Romans 5:8 says, *"God demonstrates His own love for us in this: while we were still sinners, Christ died for us."*

4) **The Response of the Son:**

Jesus' response was to obey the Father. Jesus prayed "Not my will but Your Will be done..." Jesus had surrendered His Will for the Father's Will.
1. Jesus willingly laid down His life. (**John 10:17**)
2. **John 12:32** says ..."*when I am lifted up I will draw all men to myself*".
3. He was the "Lamb of God".

(John 1:29) *..."Look, the lamb of God, who takes away the sin of the world."*

4. He asked the Father to forgive the very ones that were killing Him.

Luke 23:34 says, **"*Jesus said, "Father, forgive them, for they do not know what they are doing."*"**

5. His response was to endure death, even death on the cross because of His love for us.

Jesus could have called ten thousand angels to destroy the world and set Him free but He died alone, for you and me.

Man will try to hang on to life when death is near. But I am told that a lamb will often lick the hand of the one that is going to kill it. Jesus was that lamb that showing His love even to all that were killing Him. (This includes us)

Isaiah 53 has been said to be the Gospel according to Isaiah. In it Isaiah tells about Jesus more than 500 years before Jesus was born in a manger. Let us turn to **Isaiah 53** and read about Jesus Response.

Isaiah 53 (NIV)

¹ Who has believed our message and to whom has the arm of the LORD been revealed?

² He grew up before him like a tender shoot, and like a root out of dry ground. He had no beauty or majesty to attract us to him, nothing in his appearance that we should desire him.

³ He was despised and rejected by mankind, a man of suffering, and familiar with pain. Like one from whom people hide their faces he was despised, and we held him in low esteem.

⁴ Surely he took up our pain and bore our suffering, yet we considered him punished by God, stricken by him, and afflicted.

⁵ But he was pierced for our transgressions, he was crushed for our iniquities; the punishment that brought us peace was on him, and by his wounds we are healed.

⁶ We all, like sheep, have gone astray, each of us has turned to our own way; and the LORD has laid on him the iniquity of us all.

⁷ He was oppressed and afflicted, yet he did not open his mouth; he was led like a lamb to the slaughter, and as a sheep before its shearers is silent, so he did not open his mouth.

⁸ By oppression and judgment he was taken away. Yet who of his generation protested? For he was cut off from the land of the living; for the transgression of my people he was punished.

⁹ He was assigned a grave with the wicked, and with the rich in his death, though he had done no violence, nor was any deceit in his mouth.

¹⁰ Yet it was the LORD's will to crush him and cause him to suffer, and though the LORD makes his life an offering for sin, he will see his offspring and prolong his days, and the will of the LORD will prosper in his hand.

¹¹ After he has suffered, he will see the light of life and be satisfied; by his knowledge my righteous servant will justify many, and he will bear their iniquities. ¹² Therefore I will give him a portion among the great, and he will divide the spoils with the strong, because he poured out his life unto death, and was numbered with the transgressors. For he bore the sin of many, and made intercession for the transgressors.

Now we come to a question that everyone will have to answer.

5) **What is Your Response?**

You see the cross is not only a symbol of death; it is also the symbol of life. Eternal life is for all those that respond to God's great Love and accept God's free gift that He gave us 2000 years ago.

How do I make this symbol of death become my symbol of life?

Admit that you have done wrong, that you can't make it to heaven without God's help. The Bible tells us that we all have sinned.

Believe that God Loves You and sent His Son Jesus to take the penalty for your sin.

Accept God's free gift of eternal life in Jesus Christ. Accept God's forgiveness and Love. Ask God to send His Holy Spirit to live in you today.

Confess Jesus as Lord and believe God raised Him from the dead and you will be saved.

It is so simple to pray and accept Jesus today. Just say, *"Yes, Jesus, I surrender my will to Your Will today. I admit I have done wrong. I believe You died for my sins. I now accept Your gift of eternal life. Come take complete control of my life. I want You to be my Lord and Savior today. You come and live in me today. I want a personal relationship with you. I invite You to come in and take complete control of my life today. And now I say Thank You for coming into my life. Thank You for making a symbol of death become my symbol of life today."*

If you prayed that prayer with me today and really meant it, you now have eternal life. And I would like to give you a book that will help you to get started with your New Life in Christ.

The Spirit and the Bride say, "Come!"

"Loving God with all our heart, mind, and body."

2 Timothy 3:1 - 5 (NIV)

"But mark this: There will be terrible times in the last days. People will be lovers of themselves, lovers of money, boastful, proud, abusive, disobedient to their parents, ungrateful, unholy, without love, unforgiving, slanderous, without self-control, brutal, <u>not lovers of God - having a form of godliness but denying its power.</u> Have nothing to do with them."

Revelation 2:1-5 (NIV)

"To the angel of the church in Ephesus write:

"These are the words of Him who holds the seven stars in His right hand and walks among the seven golden lampstands: I know your deeds, your hard work and your perseverance, I know that you

cannot tolerate wicked men, that you have tested those who claim to be apostles but are not, and have found them false. You have persevered and have endured hardships for my name, and have not grown weary.

Yet I hold this against you: <u>You have forsaken your first love. Remember the height from which you have fallen! Repent and do the things you did at first.</u> If you do not repent, I will come to you and remove your lamp stand from its place."

Mark 12:30 (NIV) Jesus was asked what the Greatest Commandment was.

Jesus said in verse 30; "<u>**Love the Lord your God with all your heart and with all your soul and with all your mind and with all your strength.**</u>"

How many know that God is doing something with His Church today? How many know that God is pouring out His Spirit on His Church today and fires of revival are starting all over the world?

We are getting closer to the day that this in **Revelation 19:6-8** will take place.

Revelation 19:6-8 (NIV) *"Then I heard what sounded like a great multitude, like the roar of rushing waters and like peals of thunder, shouting: "Hallelujah! For the Lord God Almighty reigns. Let us rejoice and be glad and give Him glory!* <u>*For the wedding of the Lamb has come, and His bride has made herself ready. Fine linen, bright and clean, was given her to wear.*</u>*"*

God is calling His church <u>back to their first love</u>. He is <u>sending revival</u>. *(Fine linen)* that will <u>make us bright and clean</u>. He is <u>getting His bride</u> *(the Church)* <u>ready</u> for His return.

God has called us to be <u>Lovers of Him</u>. We are to <u>Love Him with all of our with all our heart and with all our soul and with all our mind and all our strength</u>.

This should be the desire of all who have called on the name of the Lord Jesus to be their Lord and Savior. <u>God wants to clean us</u>. God wants to <u>purify</u> us. God wants to put the <u>Fine Linen</u>, <u>bright</u> and <u>clean</u> on us. God wants to dwell in us and work through us today to bring in the Great Harvest. We can't do it without the presence and power of God in us. And we can <u>not</u> have that until we return to our first love. We need to return and Love Him with all our heart and with all our soul and with all our mind and all our strength. We have to surrender unconditionally to God's Holy Spirit to allow His Love to come in us completely so that we can Love Him completely. This kind of Love will last. The Love from God Himself dwelling in us.

Just for a moment I want each of you to imagine that tomorrow is your wedding day. **And just suppose** that the one that is to be your husband or wife for life comes to you and tells you they really love you and that they promise that they will be faithful to you and love you at least 85 to 90 percent of the time.

What would you think? 85% to 90% of the time? What about the other 10% to 15%?

Who would you be loving the other 10% to 15 %?

How would you feel about your wedding tomorrow and your husband or bride to be?

It is a total commitment. 100% It is loving God with all our heart and with all our soul and with all our mind and with all our strength. That is what God wants. It is putting God in first place in our life every day. To do this we must allow the Love of God to flow in and through us. This can only be done when each one of us totally unconditionally surrender to Him.

I believe God is calling His church to a real, on fire, personal passionate loving relationship with Him. He is calling His church to seek Him with their whole heart, mind, soul, and strength. He is calling His church to hunger and thirst after His righteousness.

I believe it is time to get rid of all the hidden sins that we have been carrying around. It is time to become pure in His sight. It is not a time to continue to go through the motion of being religious. It is a time to get a real personal passionate relationship with God. It is a time to allow God complete control of our lives. 100% It is a time to stand in His presence. It is a time to walk in Him. It is a time to listen to and obey Him.

We are going to have to surrender completely to Him and allow Him to do whatever is needed in order to get us right with Him. It is a time to become pure and clean with Him. It is a time of renewal. It is a time for a personal revival. It is a time to receive a fresh filling of His Love. It is a time to really get to know God personally and love Him intimately, not just to know about Him.

God is calling His church to a new depth of <u>total surrender, total obedience, total love</u>, and <u>total power</u>. We are at the edge of a great awakening that the world has never seen. We are at the beginning of a <u>great outpouring of His love</u> by His Holy Spirit upon us <u>to prepare us to be the pure Bride of Christ</u>. As He does this, we will see miracles again that were seen in the early church. We will see thousands coming to the Lord daily. As we spend more time putting Him first and seeking Him with our whole being, His anointing will also come and His power will work through His refined pure Church.

Are we ready to take the step of total surrender to God today? Are we ready to put God first in our life today?

Matthew 6:33 Jesus says: *"Seek first His kingdom and His righteousness, and all these things will be given to you as well."*

Revelation 22:12-17 (NIV) Jesus said,
"Behold, I am coming soon! My reward is with me, and I will give to everyone according to what he has done. I am the Alpha and the Omega, the First and the Last, the Beginning and the End.

"Blessed are those who wash their robes, that they may have the right to the tree of life and may go through the gates into the city. Outside are the dogs, those who practice magic arts, the sexually immoral, the murders, the idolaters and everyone who loves and practices falsehood.

"I, Jesus, have sent my angel to give you this testimony for the churches. I am the Root and the Offspring of David, and the bright Morning Star."

"The Spirit and the bride say, "Come!" And let him who hears say, "Come!" Whoever is thirsty, let him come; and whoever wishes, let him take the free gift of the water of life."

Today is the time to decide to really **Love our God with all our heart and with all our soul and with all our mind and all our strength. If we do the above, then and only then will we are able to love others as God wants us to. Only then will we have true revival.**

Romans 3:23 (NIV): *"For all have sinned and fall short of the glory of God."* We need to see that we have all fallen short of being perfect.

Romans 6:23 (NIV): *"For the wages of sin is death, but the gift of God is eternal life in Christ Jesus our Lord."*

Romans 5:8 (NIV): *"But God demonstrates His own love for us in this: While we were yet sinners, Christ died for us."*

John 3:16 (NIV): *"For God so loved the world that He gave His one and only Son, that whoever believes in Him shall not perish but have eternal life."*

John 14:6 (NIV): (Jesus speaking), <u>*"I am the way and the truth and the life. No one comes to the Father except through Me."*</u>

Don't be afraid of God. He loves you so much. He wants to do great things in your life. Ask Him to come into your life today and fill you with His love. Commit yourself to totally love Him with all of your heart, soul, mind, and strength.

(Matthew 7:9-11 NIV) Jesus said,
"Which of you, if his son asks for bread, will give him a stone? Or if he asks for a fish, will give him a snake? If you, then, though you are evil, know how to give good gifts to your children, how much more will

your Father in heaven give good gifts to those who ask Him!"

Admit that you have done wrong, that you can't make it to heaven without God's help. The Bible tells us that we all have sinned.

Believe that God Loves You and sent His Son Jesus to take the penalty for your sin.

Accept God's free gift of eternal life in Jesus Christ. Accept God's forgiveness and Love. Ask God to send His Holy Spirit to live in you today.

Confess Jesus as Lord and believe God raised Him from the dead and you will be saved.

Talk to God right now. He loves you and He wants you to become His child. He will listen to you. He will keep His promise to save you when you seek Him with all of your heart. He has a plan for your life. He wants to live in and through you to carry out His Will. Will you surrender to Him today? Just say, "Yes, Jesus, I surrender my will to Your Will today. I want to be born again. I want to enter into Your Kingdom. Come take complete control of my life. You come and live in me today. I don't want religion; I want a personal relationship with you. I want you Lord. I accept You not only as my Savior but also as my Lord. Make me a new creation. Send Your Holy Spirit to live in my life from this day forward. Do Your work in and through me."

In Jesus' Name, Amen.

THE GIFT OF JESUS

Luke 1:47-55 NIV

"and my spirit rejoices in God my Savior, for he has been mindful of the humble state of his servant. From now on all generations will call me blessed, for the Mighty One has done great things for me— holy is his name. His mercy extends to those who fear him, from generation to generation. He has performed mighty deeds with his arm; he has scattered those who are proud in their inmost thoughts. He has brought down rulers from their thrones but has lifted up the humble. He has filled the hungry with good things but has sent the rich away empty. He has helped his servant Israel, remembering to be merciful to Abraham and his descendants forever, just as he promised our ancestors."

God gives us many gifts. There is the gift of Unlimited Living. In that gift God gives us Unlimited Resources, Strength and Access.

There is the gift of the Relationship with Him by the gift of Spirit Filled Living. In that gift God gives us A Personal, Consuming, and An Empowering Relationship with Him by Spirit Filled Living.

There is the gift of Significance or of having a Purpose for Living. In that gift God gives us our purpose for living. We are to be like Jesus. The Bible tells us that **"Jesus was anointed by God and went around doing good and healing all who were under the power of the devil. (Acts 10:38)** The Bible also tells us that Jesus **said "As the Father has sent me, I am sending you." (John 20:21)**

In Isaiah 61 defines Jesus' Purpose as well as Ours Purpose. **Isaiah 61:1-2 (NIV)** says, *"The Spirit of the Sovereign LORD is on me, because the LORD has anointed me to proclaim good news to the poor. He has sent me to bind up the brokenhearted, to proclaim freedom for the captives and release from darkness for the prisoners, "to proclaim the year of the LORD's favor..."*

We are called to be like Jesus so our purpose is also. Yet in order for any of the gifts above to be fully activated we must receive the Greatest Gift of All, the Gift of Jesus.

Today I want to talk about the Greatest Gift Ever Given. And as I talk about the Gift of Jesus I would like you to Open up the Gift of Christmas and receive Him with gladness. Jesus!

Jesus came into the world as God's gift to mankind. And, of course, we know what He came to do. He came to save us from sin.

John 3:16 (NIV) *"For God so loved the world that He gave His one and only Son, that whoever believes in Him shall not perish but have eternal life."*

Romans 6:23 (NIV) *"For the wages of sin is death, but the gift of God is eternal life in Christ Jesus our Lord."*

We have to first Receive Jesus into our Hearts before we can really open up the other gifts that we have been talking about and are listed above.

Today let us look at some verses that most may just pass over when reading the Christmas story. **(Luke 1:47-55)** Out of these verses I am going show **three reasons Christ came into the world**. And at the same time if we can identify with any one of these then we can open up this Gift and Receive Eternal Life.

1) HE CAME FOR THE HUMBLE

(vs. 48) *"for he has been mindful of the humble state of his servant."*

(vs. 52) *"He has brought down rulers from their thrones but has lifted up the humble."*

Mary was humble. And God used her. Remember the story Jesus told in **Luke 18** about the two men that went to the temple to pray. Jesus said, *"Two men went up to the temple to pray, one a Pharisee* (a religious leader, one believed to know God) *and the other a tax collector.* (thought by many to be a thief and a liar) *The Pharisee stood up and prayed about himself: 'God, I thank you that I am not like other men - robbers, evildoers, adulterers - or even like this tax collector. I fast twice a week and give a tenth of all I get.'*

"But the tax collector stood at a distance. He would not even look up to heaven, but beat his breast and said, 'God have mercy on me, a sinner.'

"I tell you that this man, rather than the other, when home justified before God. For everyone who humbles himself will be exalted."

2) HE CAME FOR THE POOR
(vs.53) *"He has filled the hungry with good things but has sent the rich away empty."*

We are not just talking about those without money but there are many that are poor in other ways as well. **We saw in Isaiah 61 that the poor included, broken hearted, captives, all those that are hurting Physically, Spiritually, and Emotionally.**

3) HE CAME FOR THE LOST
(vs. 47) *"My soul glorifies the Lord and my spirit rejoices in God my Savior."*

In this opening statement of Mary's Song she admits that she needs a savior. Jesus came into a lost world. He came *"to seek and save what was lost."* (Luke 19:10) In fact, Jesus real name in Hebrew was "Yeshua" sometimes short for "Yahshua" which means "Yah's Salvation" or God's Salvation. (Yah is often used as a short version of God's Holy Name of "YHVH" or Yahweh)

So when people called his name Yeshua (Jesus) they were really saying there is "God's Salvation"!

Jesus did not come into the world just to:
    1) To teach us a better way,
    2) To show us how to live,
    3) To heal the sick and raise the dead,

He did do all of those things but that was not His real reason for coming. He did not come into the world to condemn the world, even though He had every right to.
Jesus came into the world to save the world. He came because we needed a savior and He Himself was God's Salvation. From the very beginning, God's plan was that Jesus would save us from our sins. Before Christ was born, an angel said to Joseph... ***"You are to give Him the name Jesus, because He will save His people from their sins."*** (Matthew 1:21)

What began in Bethlehem Away in a Manger, was finished at Calvary on the Old Rugged Cross.

Jesus died on the cross for the sins of the world, including your sins and mine. This is the greatest gift; The Gift of Jesus. It is a free gift, just reach out and receive it.

Admit that you have done wrong, that you can't make it to heaven without God's help. The Bible tells us that we all have sinned.

Believe that God Loves You and sent His Son Jesus to take the penalty for your sin.

Accept God's free gift of eternal life in Jesus Christ. Accept God's forgiveness and Love. Ask God to send His Holy Spirit to live in you today.

Confess Jesus as Lord and believe God raised Him from the dead and you will be saved.

Talk to God right now. He loves you and He wants you to become His child. He will listen to you. He will keep His promise to save you when you seek Him with all of your heart. He has a plan for your life. He wants to live in and through you to carry out His Will. Will you surrender to Him today? Just say, "Yes, Jesus, I surrender my will to Your Will today. I want to be born again. I want to enter into Your Kingdom. Come take complete control of my life. You come and live in me today. I want a personal relationship with you. I want you Lord. I accept You not only as my Savior but also as my Lord. Make me a new creation. Send Your Holy Spirit to live in my life from this day forward. Do Your work in and through me."
In Jesus' Name, Amen.

NO VACANCY

LUKE 2:1-14 NIV

"In those days Caesar Augustus issued a decree that a census should be taken of the entire Roman world. And everyone went to their own town to register.

So Joseph also went up from the town of Nazareth in Galilee to Judea, to Bethlehem the town of David, because he belonged to the house and line of David. He went there to register with Mary, who was pledged to be married to him and was expecting a child. While they were there, the time came for the baby to be born, and she gave birth to her firstborn, a son. She wrapped him in cloths and placed him in a manger, because there was no guest room available for them.

And there were shepherds living out in the fields nearby, keeping watch over their flocks at night. An angel of the Lord appeared to them, and the glory of the Lord shone around them, and they were terrified. But the angel said to them, "Do not be afraid. I bring you good news that will cause great joy for all the people. Today in the town of David a Savior has been born to you; he is the Messiah, the Lord. This will be a sign to you: You will find a baby wrapped in cloths and lying in a manger." Suddenly a great company of the heavenly host appeared with the angel, praising God and saying, "Glory to God in the highest heaven, and on earth peace to those on whom his favor rests."

Verse 7 says... *"because there was no guest room available for them."*

Have you ever gone on a Vacation trip and when it came time to find a place to stay all you saw on the signs were **"NO Vacancy"**. I remember as a kid going on vacation with my parents and seeing many or this signs before finding a place to stay for the night.

We need to realize the difference between a manger, in a *"Stable"* and an Inn or *"Guest Room"*. A stable in Israel was often a cave where the animals were kept. In the Stable would be a feeding trough for the animal food. That is a manger. That is where Jesus was born. A guest room was often that set apart room set up for guest to stay in that would have all the convenience of home. This is most likely where we would rather stay overnight instead of in a stable with the animals.

So why was there no room in the Inn? There were lots of people in the town. Others probably got there first. Remember Mary was pregnant and soon to deliver a child. They most likely had to make many stops to rest and also could not travel as fast as others. Another reason could be that maybe because they were poor. Maybe the Inn keeper was looking for a bribe. Maybe some rich folk would offer five times the normal rate to get a room. We really don't know all the reasons.

But why is there no room in many hearts for Christ today? It could be because Christ doesn't bribe us. For some of us it is not because we hate Jesus or even dislike Him but just because we are so full of other things that we turn Him away. It could be that we have filled our hearts with other things and have no room for Him. We have put up the sign "No Vacancy".

Maybe we say why read the Bible today I have got too much to do? Maybe we say why go to church I need at least one day to relax or to sleep late, or to do something else?

Why didn't the Inn Keeper have room for Joseph & Mary? I wonder if it was Caesar Augustus had wanted a room. Do you think there would have been room found or made for him? Maybe the Inn Keeper just didn't know the importance of Christ.

Most likely the Inn Keeper had never heard of Joseph, Mary, or a Christ Child. He probably didn't know the scriptures or didn't listen to the prophets or if he had listened maybe he didn't believe that God would send a Christ Child or Messiah. Or at least God would not send the Messiah on that night at his house. Maybe somewhere else at another time but just not then.

What about today? Why is it today that many people refuse to make room in their hearts for Christ?

Many people who fail to make room for Christ today simply don't believe Christ wants a room in their heart. Many don't recognize Him. They don't read the Bible or if they read it they don't believe it or they refuse to listen to the preachers and evangelist and other Christians witnessing to them. Either way they don't believe God really loves them so much to send us His one and only Son to died for us on the cross. Maybe God would send and show His love to another but not to them and not now. *But God did send His Son and He did and is showing His Love.*

Many of us have grown so accustomed to the tenants we have now in our hearts that we refuse to ask anyone to give up a room. We are more comfortable with the junk placed within us by the enemy to make a change. We may like Sin and Darkness better than Purity and Light. Most have been deceived to thinking that it really doesn't matter anyway.

Now some of us do ask for the other things to leave, but those dwelling there, being of the devil, won't just leave by asking, they put up a fight to stay and rather than fighting we just say, *"O well, keep your place, Christ will just have to stay out until I have a vacancy."* And because of this we never really know the joy of having the Spirit of God within our hearts.

So we find that Jesus was born in a stable and laid in a manger. *How did Joseph & Mary happen to secure this humble place one may ask?* I don't think they just go in and run out the cows & sheep and take over. I believe someone said, *"I don't have a guest room but I'll give you what I have... not much but if you will come in and use it you will be welcomed."* Joseph & Mary accepted the offer and the Lord Jesus was not born in a guest room but in a small corner of a stable.

This is another part of God's plan that should have great meaning for us today. Don't put Jesus off..... Yes it would be great to give Him the best room in our house, but whatever you do, don't leave Him out in the cold. <u>Give Him whatever room you can.</u> Let Him come in. Let the Light of the World into your life. You may just find that when Light comes in, Darkness will leave. Maybe we are filled up with worldly things but if we look closely we should find a little, even dirty room left somewhere inside of us that is available. I know we feel that this is not good enough for Christ, and it's not perfect but if that's all we have now, let us ask Him to come in. Let us welcome Him in even to this humble place like a stable that most likely has the smell of barn.

If we would just invite Him into whatever place we have we will be surprised because He will come in. We don't have to wait until the room is cleaned up. He just wants to come in and He will help do the cleaning. His Holy Spirit is really good at cleaning us up when we allow

Him to. What a difference He will make in our life when we just make room for Him.

Let Him in today and soon we will find that He has helped us to evict those undesirable tenants who have taken so much of our lives and love. *Yes as the coming of Christ into the world has made a difference, the coming of Christ into our hearts will also make a difference.*

No matter who you are or how bad you think you are; I ask you let Him in today? Maybe just a small corner of your life but let Him come in.

And if Christ is already in your life. Look around and see just how much room have you given to Him? Are you preparing a larger, more beautiful room for Him? Give it all to Him today. Emanuel means "God with us". He is at the door knocking to come in. Let us all open the door and make room for Emanuel to fill us today.

"Heavenly Father, I surrender my will to Your Will today. I want to be born again. I want to enter into Your Kingdom. Come take complete control of my life. You come and live in me today. I want a personal relationship with you. I want you Lord. Emanuel, (God with us), yes I want you to be with me. I accept You not only as my

Savior but also as my Lord. Make me a new creation. Send Your Holy Spirit to live in my life from this day forward. Do Your work in and through me." In Your Holy Name I pray. Amen.

BE LIKE AN EAGLE

Isaiah 40:31 (*The Amplified Bible*)

"But those who wait for the Lord [who expect, look for, and hope in Him] shall change and renew their strength and power; they shall lift their wings and mount up [close to God] as eagles [mount up to the sun]; they shall run and not be weary, they shall walk and not faint or become tired."

What can we learn from this verse and how can we apply it as we head toward revival? Are we waiting for the Lord? Are we expecting the Lord to show up? Are we looking for Him to show up? Are we putting our hope in Him?

If so, then we shall change (exchange) and renew our strength and power with his strength and power. We will be able to spread out our wings and soar close to God as an eagle soars up in the sky. We will run and not be weary; we will walk and not faint or become tired.

God is planning to do mighty things in our area. We are getting closer and closer to the harvest of harvest. The question is, "Will we allow Him to use us?"

Are we waiting for the Lord?
Are we expecting the Lord to show up?
Are we looking for Him to show up?
Are we putting our hope in Him?

If we are then He will renew us with His power and strength and be able to do mighty things through us to make a difference in this region.

What else can we learn from looking at an eagle that will help us understand how God can and will use us as we do what he desires.

Let us look at 4 different things eagle do that we can apply to get ready for the next mighty move of God.

173

FIRST: Habakkuk 1:8 (NKJV) *In this verse we see that it says that the eagle "...fly as the eagle that hastens to eat."*

The eagle has a keen eye and is ready to zoom down to catch its prey when it is hungry. We too should be hungry for more of God. We should be as the eagle that is alert and ready and looking for more of God and when we see it we should zoom down to receive more of God as if our survival depended on it. We need to be <u>always hungry for more of God and looking and seeking more of Him.</u>

SECOND: Job 39:27-28 (NKJV) *"Does the eagle mount up at your command, And make its nest on high? It dwells on the rock, and resides on the crag of the rock and the stronghold."*

The eagle dwells on the rock. It makes its nest on high places. We are to dwell on the Rock! Jesus Christ. He is our Rock and our Salvation. Our homes need to be in Him. Jesus is the solid foundation. All other ground is sinking sand. <u>Always stand on the Rock of Jesus !</u>

THIRD: Proverbs 23:5 (NKJV) *"Will you set your eyes on that which is not? For riches certainly make* *themselves wings; They fly away like an eagle toward heaven."*

What do we have our eyes on? Don't put your eyes on things that don't really matter. Keep your eyes on Jesus. Keep our eyes on Heaven. **"Seek ye first the Kingdom of God and His righteous..."** <u>Keep our eyes on Jesus, not on things that don't really matter.</u>

<u>FORTH</u>: Jeremiah 48:40 (NKJV) **"For thus says the Lord: "Behold, one shall fly like an eagle, And spread his wings over Moab."**

Have you ever seen an eagle or a hawk fly? It can spread its wings and soar and soar and soar without flapping its wings. Why because it is riding on the wind. It has surrendered to the wind. We need to learn surrender completely to the Wind of the Holy Spirit. As we do surrender to Him, He will carry us to new highs. We will soar and not become weary. We will walk in His Spirit and not faint or become tired.

As the eagle lifts its wings in surrender we can lift our hands in surrender to Him. <u>Yes, we need to Completely Surrender to the Wind of the Holy Spirit.</u>

Review: **"4 ways to be like an eagle"**

1) Always hungry for more of God and looking and seeking more of Him.

2) Always stand on the Rock of Jesus !

3) Keep our eyes on Jesus, not on things that don't really matter.

4) Yes, we need to Completely Surrender to the Wind of the Holy Spirit.

Isaiah 40:31 (*The Amplified Bible*)

"But those who wait for the Lord [who expect, look for, and hope in Him] shall change and renew their strength and power; they shall lift their wings and mount up [close to God] as eagles [mount up to the sun]; they shall run and not be weary, they shall walk and not faint or become tired.

Are we waiting for the Lord?

Are we expecting the Lord to show up?

Are we looking for Him to show up?

Are we putting our hope in Him?

God Loves You so much He sent His Only Son Jesus Christ to die on the cross just for You. He is a God of Love and He is just waiting for You to Turn to Him and Surrender to Him. He Loves You and He will forgive all of Your sins and set You free to Soar like an Eagle.

The River of Life

Revelation 22:1-2, & 17

(1-2) "Then the angel showed me the river of the water of life, as clear as crystal, flowing from the throne of God and of the Lamb down the middle of the great street of the city. On each side of the river stood the tree of life, bearing twelve crops of fruit, yielding its fruit every month. And the leaves of the tree are for the healing of the nations."

(17) "The Spirit and the bride say, "Come!" And let him who hears say, "Come!" Whoever is thirsty, let him come; and whoever wishes, let him take the free gift of the water of life."

This is the River of Life that is coming. But we can enjoy part of this River today.

In **Acts 2:17-18** we can read:

"In the last days, God says, I will pour out my Spirit on all people. Your sons and daughters will prophesy, your young men will see visions, your old men will dream dreams. Even on my servants, both men and women, I will pour out my Spirit in those days, and they will prophesy."

God is starting to pour out His Spirit all over the world today. He is pouring out that Water of Life, that Living Water for all who are thirsty. Are You Thirsty? Will this year be the year we jump in the River and Receive whatever God has for us? Will this year be the year we bring the River to others? Will this year be the year that we make a difference?

What do I believe God wants to say to the Church today? **Luke 5:1-10** says, *"One day as Jesus was standing by the Sea of Galilee, with the people crowding around him and listening to the word of God, he saw at the water's edge two boats, left there by the fishermen,* who were washing their nets. He got into one of the boats, the one belonging to Simon, and asked him to put out a little from shore. Then he sat down and taught the people from the boat."

When he had finished speaking, he said to Simon, "Put out into deep water, and let down the nets for a catch."

Simon answered, "Master, we've worked hard all night and haven't caught anything. But because you say so, I will let down the nets."

When they had done so, they caught such a large number of fish that their nets began to break. So they signaled their partners in the other boat to come and help them, and they came and filled both boats so full that they began to sink."

When Simon Peter saw this, he fell at Jesus' knees and said, "Go away from me, Lord; I am a sinful man!" For he and all his companions were astonished at the catch of fish they had taken, and so were James and John, the sons of Zebedee, Simon's partners."

Then Jesus said to Simon, "Don't be afraid; from now on you will catch men."

Jesus is telling us today to **"Put out into deep water"**.
"It is time to put out into the deep water". Now is not the time to just play around the water's edge. It is time to get busy and jump into to the River and Do the work He has called us to do.

How can we apply these verses to the Church today?
Let us look at four ways:

1) Much of the Church is standing around at the waters edge.

Much of the Church is standing around the waters edge washing our nets. Much of the Church has stopped doing what it was called to do. Some of the Church has been playing at their little water hole for so long that the River has changed course and now they are just playing in a pond with no moving water in it. A dead stagnate pond. They may say to others passing by "Come and play in our pond", but their pond has no life. The Water of Life has stooped flowing there years ago.

Some have followed the River as it moved but they are still playing at the edge of the River of Life. They say, "It's fun here at the edge and safe too". "We can walk with our feet in the cool water." "We can reach down and take a sip when we get thirsty." "It's fun in our little pool here at the edge of the river." But they will not be able to catch the Big Harvest to Come because they will not go into the deep.

2) Much of the Church is still doing things the same old way even if they no longer work.

Much of the Church is just standing around talking about how we have been fishing all night and have caught nothing. Much of the Church is telling the old fish stories of the good old days when fishing was much better. Yet not planning to change our method. They say, "We know that the best time to fish is at night. This is the way our fathers fished and their father before them. And we are going to do it the same old way too." But they fished all night and caught nothing.

3) But Thank the Lord that some of the Church is listening to Jesus and obeying Him even if it doesn't make sense. Jesus is saying, "Put out into deep water, and let down the nets for a catch."

Now is the time to trust Him and obey Him if we want to make a difference. He is saying the night is over. It is a new day, and today I want you to put out into the deep water because it is nearing the time of the Great Harvest.

The old way of fishing is not working for the Great Harvest time that is coming. You must do things differently. You must go out into the deep. You must take a chance and do things differently in order to have a big catch. Go out into the Deep Water.

4) Don't be a Church to try to hog what God is doing, but share it for it is His Harvest.

Don't be a Church that thinks that they are making it happen when the Spirit comes in power and the Harvest starts to come in. <u>Don't</u> be overly <u>Proud</u>, but <u>be Humble</u>, and <u>Give God All The Credit</u>. We are to surrender to Jesus completely. We are to drink in the Living Water. We are to soak up the Holy Spirit just as a sponge soaks up water. We need renewal, refreshing and revival in this year. Then the living water will flow from within us to those around us.

John 7:21 37-38 Jesus says: *"If anyone is thirsty, let him come to me and drink. Whoever believes in me as the Scripture has said, streams of living water will flow from within him."*

Are you thirsty? He says to come and drink. Soak in Him. And Go out into the Deep Water and make a Difference.

Where are You Today? Come to Him today and let Him Fill You with Living Water.

Meet the TATOR Family

This is a Children Sermon that my Father, (Rev. Floyd Vernon Chandler, Jr.), use to do. He would spread it out over many weeks to meet all of the Tator family, but I will introduce the whole family to you today.

Maw and Paw Tator. Now even though Maw and Paw are just ordinary Tators, it is amazing how their children turn out. It is much like the Church today. It was started out pure and holy but as time went by it has been corrupted just like the Tator family. And God wants to renew it today. So what can we learned from the Tator family and what do we need to do to correct the problems within God's Church today?

Maw and Paw Tator was doing OK by themselves and then they had a baby. They named their first child **Spec**. **Spec Tator.**

Now **Spec Tator** was just that. Spectators always just seem to watch without taking an active role. Spectator would love to watch the Holy Spirit doing things, but they never seemed to take an active role in doing what they saw God do. There is a lot of Spectators in the church today. They love to look at God moving either in church or even on TV, but they are not doing it.

The devil has even deceived many of these Spectators so that they think because they see something it means that they are doing it. But to watch God fill others with the Holy Spirit and thinking that God is doing it to you, *(without coming forward to be filled yourself)*, is a little like watching a race either on TV or at the race track and going away telling others that you won the race. A spectator only watches the race. They never win. They are really never even in the race. Do we have Spectators here in our church? Is it you? **James 1:22** says, **"Do not merely listen to the word, and so deceive yourselves. Do what it says."** **James 2:26** says **"As the body without the spirit is dead, so faith without deeds is dead."** God does not need Spectators in His Church today.

Next came along **Commen Tator.** Now the Commentator is very close to Spectator. But a Commentator is one that is always talking about what they see. They also don't take an active role yet they often talk like they are in the center of what is going on. They are always reporting, analyzing, evaluating, yet never really doing something to improve things. Often they are the ones that will look for someone to say something that may be interpreted wrong so that they can jump on it and make a big deal about the little things, while missing the Big picture itself. A Commentator will often look for an audience to tell their agenda to. And then they will talk you to death about the way they see things. Often they will leave God and His Will out of the picture. After all they are more interested in themselves and having an audience then in doing what God wants. Do we have Commentators here in our church? Is it you? **James 3: 5-6** says, *"Likewise the tongue is a small part of the body, but it makes great boasts. Consider what a great forest is set on fire by a small spark. The tongue also is a fire, a world of evil among the parts of the body. It corrupts the whole person, sets the whole course of his life on fire, and is itself set on fire by hell."* God does not need any Commentators in His Church today.

Next came along **Hesi Tator.** You know about Hesitator. Those are the ones that mean well but they will always wait to later to respond. The Hesitators in the church will sit through an altar call, knowing that they need to go forward for prayer. And then maybe after church they may come up and say *"God was really speaking to me today will you pray for me."* Or worse yet they will go home without even asking for prayer. Satan loves the Hesitators. Hell is full of them. They often think that if they will just wait a little while longer things will work out and everything will be OK. They will often say that they want to get saved or deal with a sin but they listen to Satan and say that they will get things right later, but not today, not right now. Do we have Hesitators here in our church? Is it you? **2 Corinthians 6:2** says, ***"...now is the time of God's favor, now is the day of salvation."*** See each person is not even promised another heartbeat. The next breath you take could be your last. God does not want Hesitators in His Church today. Time is too short to put off following God's Will.

Next we have little **Imi Tator.** We have all known Imitators. Some of us see one every morning when we look in the mirror. Many people today play church. They play at being a Christian. They are only Imitators, a fake, not really doing or even caring to do God's Will but they are just playing a game. They will often try to impress others to think that they are pure and holy. But they can't fool God. An Imitator is often like a cancer cell. At first it may look fairly normal but it don't belong within the body. As is grows it starts to take control and even kill the other organs around it. It cares not for the other organs health or the health of the body as a whole. It is only imitating a good cell. It's real purpose is to kill and destroy the other good cells and organs and eventually to kill the body itself. Do we have Imitators here in our church? Is it you? **1 Peter 1:16** God says through Peter, "***Be Holy because I am Holy."*** God does not want Imitators in His Church. He wants real Christians. He is tired of fake ones only doing their own thing.

Then we have **Agi Tator**. Agitators are the ones that are always stirring up people in an unfavorable way. They are always stirring up, agitating them. They will often try to stir people up against others. God wants us to live in peace. To seek His Will and His purpose for His Church, but the Agitator will stir people up for their own will and purpose. They love to cause divisions in the church. Do we have Agitators here in our church? Is it you? **Romans 16:17-18** says, *"**I urge you, brothers, to watch out for those who cause divisions and put obstacles in your way that are contrary to the teaching you have learned.***

Keep away from them. For such people are not serving our Lord Christ, but their own appetites. By smooth talk and flattery they deceive the minds of naive people." God does not want Agitators in His Church Today.

Next we have **Dic Tator.** A Dictator in a church will always want to be in control. They believe that they own the church and everyone must follow them and their wishes or else. They really feel that they are the Head of the Church, not Jesus Christ. They don't feel comfortable in other churches that they can't get control of. They are like a little Saddam Hussein, or Adolph Hitler, that want everyone to bow down to their every wish and demand. They do not want God's Will; they are only interested in pleasing themselves. They are always dictating to others. Do we have Dictators here in our church? Is it you? In **Ephesians 1:22** we are told that *"Christ is the Head of the Church".* See God establishes different authorities for different purposes. **Romans 13:1-2,** says, *"Everyone must submit himself to the governing authorities, for there is no authority except that which God has established. The authorities that exit have been established by God. Consequently, he who rebels against the authority is rebelling against what God has instituted, and those who do so will bring judgment on*

themselves." **Hebrews 13:17** reminds use to, *"**Obey your leaders and submit to their authority. They keep watch over you as men who must give an account. Obey them so that their work will be a joy, not a burden, for that would be of no advantage to you.**"*
God does not want Dictators in His Church today.

And finally Maw and Paw Tator had **Sweet Tator.** Sweet Tator is different as you can see. Sweet Tator loved all it's brother and sister tators, even when they acted poorly. A Sweet Tator would pray, *"not my will but God's Will be done."* A Sweet Tator will lay down it's life for a friend. A Sweet Tator goes around doing good. We should all be Sweet Tators. **When people look at each of us, they should notice the difference in us. They should see Jesus in us.** Not a Spectator. Not a Commentator. Not a Hesitator. Not an Imitator. Not an Agitator and not a Dictator. **They should see Jesus.**

God want us all to be Sweet Tators. God wants us to go around, like Jesus and do good. He wants us full of His Peace and Love. He wants us seeking His Will and purpose, not our own. He wants us to love each other even as Christ has loved us.

No matter whom we are today. We may have notice a little of ourselves in each of the other Tators mentioned, but today God has provided a chance to get rid of the bad parts of the Tator and to become a completely new Sweet Tator.

2 Corinthians 5:17 says, *"Therefore, if anyone is in Christ, he is a new creation; the old has gone, the new has come!"*

God wants to make each of us new today! Today does not have to be the end. It can be the new beginning of new life In Christ. If you will truly surrender your will to His Will. God loves each of you so much and He still wants to use each of you to advance His kingdom in our community and He wants each of you to continue to grow and mature within His Body in this community. **It is all up to you!**

WINNING THE SPIRITUAL BATTLE

(Ephesians 6:10-18 NIV) "Finally, be strong in the Lord and in his mighty power. Put on the full armor of God, so that you can take your stand against the devil's schemes. For our struggle is not against flesh and blood, but against the rulers, against the authorities, against the powers of this dark world and against the spiritual forces of evil in the heavenly realms. Therefore put on the full armor of God, so that when the day of evil comes, you may be able to stand your ground, and after you have done everything, to stand. Stand firm then, with the belt of truth buckled around your waist, with the breastplate of righteousness in place, and with your feet fitted with the readiness that comes from the gospel of peace. In addition to all this, take up the shield of faith, with which you can

extinguish all the flaming arrows of the evil one. Take the helmet of salvation and the sword of the Spirit, which is the word of God. And pray in the Spirit on all occasions with all kinds of prayers and requests. With this in mind, be alert and always keep on praying for all the Lord's people."

A spiritual war requires spiritual weapons. In Ephesians 6:10-18, Paul describes the spiritual armor of God. We choose to put on each piece by faith.

1) ***The helmet of salvation*** protects our minds, Satan's primary target. As we put on the helmet of Salvation and ask the Lord to make His thoughts our thoughts, we respond with the mind of Christ to the enemy's attacks.

2) ***The breastplate of righteousness*** protects our emotions and helps us counter the temptations of Satan with the truth of God. Our feelings constantly change. By asking God to substitute His truth for our feelings, we see things from His infinite viewpoint. We realize who we are in Christ and the power we have in His name over shifting tides of emotion and circumstance.

3) ***The girdle (belt) of truth*** protects us from Satan's deception. The only place to find truth is in God's Word.

Ask God to work His truth into your heart be meditating on and memorizing His Word. Truth equips the saint of God for the spiritual battle.

4) *The sandals (shoes) of peace* enable us to become peacemakers for God. The Bible says: "Blessed are the peacemakers for shall be called sons of God". (Matt. 5:9) Ask God to help you recognize the value of receiving and extending peace by faith daily. As ambassadors for Christ, we share His message of reconciliation through faith in Jesus Christ. A peacemaker resolves conflicts, not creates them.

5) *The shield of faith* covers us from the fiery attacks of the enemy. The shield Paul described completely covered the warrior. No matter how ferocious the attack, the shield of faith provides safe cover for the child of God. The shield of faith defuses two of Satan's most deadly weapons - unbelief and doubt.

6) *The sword of the Spirit* is the Word of God. It is the only weapon that can be used offensively and defensively. Find a particular passage of Scripture that pertains to your need, claim its promises, and stand firm in the faith.

Spiritual warfare is a daily battle. Put on the spiritual armor of God each morning. At first it may seem awkward, but it is preparations for eventual victory and great rejoicing. Remember who you are in Christ. Remember that because you are in Him, you are victorious. So let us prepare and go out and advance the Kingdom of God. Let us bring the Light of Jesus into our community and as we bring in His Light the darkness will flee. We will make a difference within the Kingdom!

THERE IS A REAL WAR GOING ON

(Ephesians 6:10-18 NIV) "Finally, be strong in the Lord and in his mighty power. Put on the full armor of God, so that you can take your stand against the devil's schemes. For our struggle is not against flesh and blood, but against the rulers, against the authorities, against the powers of this dark world and against the spiritual forces of evil in the heavenly realms. Therefore put on the full armor of God, so that when the day of evil comes, you may be able to stand your ground, and after you have done everything, to stand. Stand firm then, with the belt of truth buckled around your waist, with the breastplate of righteousness in place, and with your feet fitted with the readiness that

comes from the gospel of peace. In addition to all this, take up the shield of faith, with which you can extinguish all the flaming arrows of the evil one. Take the helmet of salvation and the sword of the Spirit, which is the word of God.

And pray in the Spirit on all occasions with all kinds of prayers and requests. With this in mind, be alert and always keep on praying for all the Lord's people."

The Bible tells us in **1 Peter 5:8-9** to: *"Be self-controlled and <u>alert</u>. Your enemy the devil prowls around like a roaring lion looking for someone to devour. Resist him, standing firm in the faith, because you know that your brothers throughout the world are undergoing the same kind of sufferings."*

One way we can be "<u>alert</u>" is to know a little how Satan and his evil demons operate so we can know what to look out for. And then we need to know who we are and how to put on the Full Armor of God so that we can not only stand but also advance the Kingdom of God.

1) <u>Satan wants us to doubt the Word of God.</u>
Gen. 3:1 *"...Did God really say, 'You must not eat from any tree in the garden'?"* Satan started then to

twist and cause doubt the Word of God and he is still doing it today.

2) Satan wants us to distract us from spiritual things.

He will direct our focus on material, trivial, and selfish desires. Often he will put trivial things in our schedule so that our schedule is so full that we have little time left for God.

3) Satan wants to disable us in the Lord's service.

He will always try to damage our testimony. He will often tempt us and cause us to say and do things that we should not do as a Christian. Then when we try to witness to someone they may often see a hypocrite. Saying we are a Christian but looking and acting like a devil.

4) Satan wants to destroy us physically.

He often will try to enslave us through a physical snare that leaves us bound up and helpless. Alcohol and drugs are just two of his devices. Many illness and sicknesses Satan has placed upon us to destroy us.

5) Satan uses primary "Deception".

a) One of Satan's favorite means of deception is to minimize the consequences of sin. Or to make us think we can get by with sin. *"... For whatever a man sows, this he will also reap..." Galatians 6:7*

b) Another deception of the enemy is to tell us that we can lust or desire something or someone without taking a step toward sin. *"...after desire has conceived, it gives birth to sin; and sin, when it is full-grown, gives birth to death." James 1:15*

c) Satan also misleads us to believe we can pursue what the world values and remain pure in Christ at the same time. *"Bad company corrupts good character." 1 Corinthians 15:33*

Just for an example one day take a clear glass of water and add a few drops of food coloring in the clean water. See what happens. The water gets colored. Same is true if you added dirt or bacteria to water. Would you want to drink the water after adding dirt, bacteria or even raw sewage in a glass of water?

d) Satan often leads us to desire the world's wisdom instead of His wisdom. *"Seek first His kingdom and His righteousness..." Matt. 6:33*

e) Satan deceives by never talking about the hurt, pain, broken hearts and devastation that come from decisions made apart from God's truth.

f) Satan's ultimate deception is unbelief in the Person and work of Jesus Christ. Eternal life cannot be received apart from faith in the sacrificial, all-sufficient, atoning death of Jesus Christ. **Acts 4:12** says, *"there is no other name under heaven given to men by which we must be saved."*

WE ARE TO PUT ON THE FULL ARMOR OF GOD.

1) *The helmet of salvation*
2) *The breastplate of righteousness*
3) *The girdle (belt) of truth*
4) *The sandals (shoes) of peace*
5) *The shield of faith*
6) *The sword of the Spirit*

Today I challenge each of us to start putting on the Full Armor of God each and every day. They will make a difference not only in our lives but also in the whole community as we advance the Kingdom of God.

What Now ?

John 21:3 *"I'm going to fish," Simon Peter told them, and they said, "We'll go with you." So they went out and got into the boat, but that night they caught nothing."*

Peter said, **"I'm going out to fish."** Now there is nothing wrong in going out to fish, unless God has called you to do something much greater. You see, **Jesus had already told Peter that for now own he would be catching men, not fish.** (Luke 5:10)

Jesus had already called Peter to go out and make a difference in the world. Yet, Peter, even after spending more than 3 years with Jesus. After not only seeing Jesus do many miracles but also **after Jesus had given them** the power and authority to drive out all demons and to cure diseases, and sent them out to preach the kingdom of God and to heal the sick. And they did go out from village to village, preaching the gospel and healing people everywhere. (Luke 9)

Even after seeing Jesus die on the cross and three day latter raise from the dead. **Peter decided to go back to what he was doing before.** He said "I'm going out to fish." Peter had decided to go and do what he was doing before Jesus had called him to make a difference. And we see that they fished all night and caught nothing.

We to have been called to make a difference! We to have been given authority to make a difference!

Matthew 28:20 *"All authority in heaven and on earth has been given to me. Therefore go and make disciples of all nations, baptizing them in the name of the Father and of the Son and of the Holy Spirit, and teaching them to obey everything I have commanded you. And surely I am with you always, to the very end of the age."*

It says, **"teaching them to obey everything I have commanded."** He had commanded His disciples to do the works that He did. Not in their own power **but He promised that He would be with them.** The Holy Spirit would do the work through them.

Today we have a decision to make. What are we going to do? **Are we to go ahead and do and be the difference?** -or- **Are we going to go back to what we were comfortable with before?**

If we decide to go forward with Christ full of the power of the Holy Spirit, we will see **that "All things are possible with God."** We will be able to say, **"I can do all things through Christ".** We will start to see and experience the power of God flowing in and through us to make a difference in the Kingdom of God.

But, if we chose not to do what He has called us to do, then we will fish all night and catch nothing. **This is an important day for this church**. This is an important day for this community. This is an important day for the region. Today is a new day for each of us and if chose to go own and follow Jesus, we will make a difference. If we chose to go back to the way we were before, we will not make any difference at all. In **Luke 9:62** Jesus said, "*No one who* *puts his hand to the plow and looks back is fit for service in the kingdom of God."*

Philippians 3:13-14 Paul says, *"...Forgetting what is behind and straining toward what is ahead, I press on toward the goal to win the prize for which God has called me in Christ Jesus."*

God wants us to forget what is behind and to press toward the goal. I believe that we are in the last days. **2 Timothy 3:5** tells us that in the last days that people will *"***a form of godliness but denying its power***".* Then it gives us a warning, "***Have nothing to do with them."***

For the most part this had been a picture of the Church. But today God is calling His people to **stop playing church and to start being the Church**. God is calling His people to stand up and to walk in faith and make a difference.

In **John 15:16** Jesus says, "***You did not choose me, but I chose you and appointed you to go and bear fruit - fruit that will last."* God has chosen this church for a reason.** He has anointed us for a purpose. He wants us to make a difference in this community. Out of all the ones that He could have chosen, He chose you. He chose us. He chose us. Will we continue to follow Him or will we retreat and go back to the way we fished before and not make a difference?

It is time for each of us to stand up, and completely surrender to God and allow Him to empower us to advance His Kingdom by the power and guidance of the Holy Spirit. It is a time to keep on keeping on. It is a time to seek more of Him.

Father today Let Your Glory Fall, Let Your Kingdom Come, Let Your Will Be Done, Let the Whole Earth See The Glory Of Your Son, The Church In Victory!

LEONARD MCDONALD SHOWED ME MORE OF WHAT GOD AND TRUE LOVE REALLY IS

1 John 4:8 (NIV) *"Whoever does not love does not know God, because God is love."*

Leonard was a man full of Love. A man full of God because God is Love and God was living in Leonard and flowing out of him to those around him.

Matthew 22:36-40 (NIV) Jesus was asked, *"Teacher, which is the greatest commandment in the Law?" Jesus replied: "'Love the Lord your God with all your heart and with all your soul and with all your mind.' This is the first and greatest commandment. And the second is like it: 'Love your neighbor as yourself.' All* *the Law and the Prophets hang on these two commandments."*

In all the 28 plus years I have had the privilege of knowing Leonard as both a **good friend** and as **my father.** I cannot ever remember a time when he did not express or ever live out the **greatest commandments of Loving God and Loving Others.**

1 Thessalonians 5:17 (King James Version) *The Bible tells us to "Pray without ceasing."*

Leonard's motto for life was to pray always. I will always remember one time, this past week, when I asked Leonard about praying he responded **"… I am always praying …"** I believe Leonard had that special oneness with God so that each and every day he was praying without ceasing.

Philippians 4:7 (NIV) *"And the peace of God, which transcends all understanding, will guard your hearts and your minds in Christ Jesus."*

Leonard a man with the Peace of God in him….

I have truly been blessed by Leonard and he has taught me not only in words, but with his actions and deeds, what True Love is. As a mirror will reflect the light and warmth of the Sun, Leonard reflects the Love of God and of His Son Jesus Christ.

I will always remember many of the special times I have shared with Leonard but there is one special time I want to share with you. Sunday morning a week ago, April 3, 2011, one week before Leonard went to be with the LORD. I was truly blessed to spend some time alone with Leonard in his hospital room "***316***", (which I also believe is another witness and promise given to us in the Bible)

John 3:16 (NIV) *"For God so loved the world that he gave his one and only Son, that whoever believes in him shall not perish but have eternal life."*

In that hospital room, Sunday morning, we had a special time alone to talk and pray. During that time I asked him if he wanted me to pray for him. And as his live motto, he assured me that he has been and always is praying. But I then asked if I could pray with him out loud with him and I asked him how he wanted me to focus my prayer for him. He said, *"Don't prayer for me because I know where I am going when God decides it is time to take me Home, my prayer if for my family and those I will be leaving behind. I pray for my family to continue to love for, to care for and to live in love and peace with each other after I am gone...."*

Leonard's main focus and prayer was for us.

His main desire was that the same Love of God in him would also be in and flow through each of us.

As he said that my thoughts went to Jesus when he prayed for us as well and it reminded me again how Leonard always reflected the Love of God even when he also knew his time was getting short. After we prayed my thoughts went to the follow Scripture...

John 17:20-26 (NIV) Jesus Prays for All Believers

"My prayer is not for them alone. I pray also for those who will believe in me through their message, that all of them may be one, Father, just as you are in me and I am in you. May they also be in us so that the world may believe that you have sent me. I have given them the glory that you gave me, that they may be one

as we are one— I in them and you in me—so that they may be brought to complete unity. Then the world will know that you sent me and have loved them even as you have loved me.

"Father, I want those you have given me to be with me where I am, and to see my glory, the glory you have given me because you loved me before the creation of the world. "Righteous Father, though the world does not know you, I know you, and they know that you have sent me. I have made you known to them, and will continue to make you known in order that the love you have for me may be in them and that I myself may be in them."

Leonard's prayer reflected

the heart and prayer of Jesus

Then I will also remember the last thing Leonard said to me this past Sunday as I told him I loved him, he responded, *"I love you too, just as one of my own."*

Another reflection of God the Father. God loves each of us so much. He claims us as His own and His desire is for each of us to have that close fellowship and relationship with Him as His Child.

God's desire is for His Love to be in us and flow through us to others. His desire is for us to reflect His Love and His Son just like Leonard did.

Thank you Leonard, Thank you my Father for SHOWING ME MORE OF WHAT GOD AND TRUE LOVE REALLY IS LIKE.

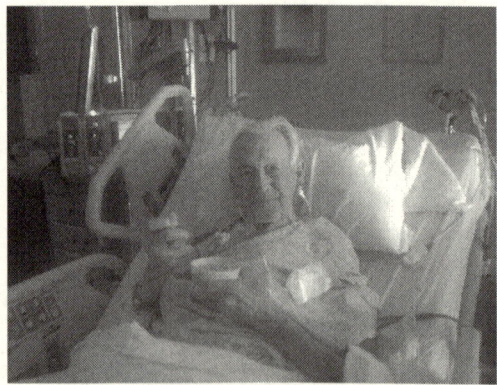

Picture on the right was taken just one day before going to be with the LORD on April 10, 2011 at over 90 years of age. Notice his smile. He knew his LORD and where he was going. You can be sure too.

Picture of my father in Israel in 1971

Picture of my brother and I in Israel in 1998

A MOTHER'S FAITH MAKES A DIFFERENCE

Ledora (Betty) McDonald (Picture 1974)

Nanny Broome (1968)    *Nanny Chandler (1951)*

(2 Timothy 1:5-6 My Version) *"I am reminded of your sincere faith, which first lived in your grandmothers Nanny Broome and Nanny Chandler and in your mother Ledora (Betty) McDonald and, I am persuaded, now lives in you also. For this reason I remind you to fan into flame the gift of God, which is in you through the laying on of my hands."*

I Love You and Thank You All!

Background and Information
About
Joseph Albert Chandler:

"A talmid is not above his rabbi; but each one, when he is fully trained, will be like his rabbi." (Luke 6:40 CJB)

At the time of the writing of this edition of this book, Joseph Chandler is the director of In Him Ministries. He is ordained with The Missionary Church International and also a member of the Apostolic Network of Global Awakening.

As the LORD leads and opens doors, Joseph Chandler ministers in teaching the Word of God while sharing the Supernatural Love of God the Father. He also shares that same Love in the Anointing while providing Soaking Prayer for others. During these times of prayer, the Power of God goes through him to touch and change the lives of others.

His desire and calling is to
"Help Others to Reach
Their Full Potential In Messiah!"

Here is a little of my background.

My father, Rev. Floyd Vernon Chandler, Jr., was a Methodist Minister for more than 30 years. So I was raised within that background. My church background includes the Methodist Church where my father served as minister. I first received the LORD in a personal relationship in 1972 within the Methodist Church. After marrying in 1983 to my wonderful wife Deidra, God guided me to work with a variety of other groups including Methodist, Baptist, and Independent Christian Fellowships with a Vineyard style, and Pentecostal. He has also guided us to work with some Messianic and Jewish groups throughout the years. All of which were a learning experience.

God has blessed my wife, Deidra and me with three children: Ashley, Sarah and Joey. I praise God for my family. They truly are a blessing given from above. All of our children have now grown up into adulthood with their own challenges and adventures of their own. Within our family background we also have Jewish and Native American roots as well which added to our education as we search out these connections but also shared it with our children as we learned and grew together on our journey and gained respect and love each "Tribe" that help make up our "Tribe" within the Body of Messiah.

In the late 1980's I felt God was calling me into the ministry of some sort. I just was not sure what kind it would be. The United Methodist wanted a Regional Accredited Bachelor degree to start the entry process, which I did not have at that time, so I started preparing the only way I knew how by taking Bible courses. In 1990 I completed an Advanced Bible Studies Diploma from Liberty University and we started looking at Village Missions as a possible place to serve. At one time we were even Candidates and set to go to Candidate School with Village Missions when my father passed away the Fall of 1993 just a month or two before the school.

After my father passed, we decided to wait for a year and just seek the LORD where he had already placed us at before decided what to do. During that time we continued to serve in the church where God had placed us as well as hosting a home group that met at our home. Then in 1995 I was hit with the Power of the Holy Spirit through the ministry of Clark Taylor from Australia. Later that year, 1995, I was ordained with The Missionary Church International (The Missionary Methodist Church) and started In Him Ministries. Since then I have served as a Pastor in 1996-1998, a Youth Pastor in 1999-2000, a Messianic Fellowship Leader as well as an Emergency Responder Chaplain the years afterwards.

"Catch the Vision"

"Make a difference in our world by surrendering our wills to God's Will. Allowing God to empower us to advance His Kingdom by proclaiming the Gospel of Jesus the Messiah, not only in word, but with actions and deeds by the power and guidance of the Holy Spirit."

I have traveled to and spent several days at Toronto Canada, Pensacola Florida and to Lakeland Florida during the different outpourings to catch some of the anointing of what God is doing and give it to others. I have completed Catch the Fire Ministries "Soaking In His Presence" School. I have also been blessed to attend "Kingdom Foundations; "A School of Healing and Impartation" from Global Awakening. Many different anointed ministers have prayed for and imparted to me to receive more of God's anointing for ministry during the years. With each deposit, I knew God was doing and preparing for the "greater than" to be released to those he allowed me to minister to.

I traveled to Israel in 1998 to gain a better understanding of Israel, Jewish People and the life and ministry of Jesus. Part of that journey of seeking the roots of our faith took us into Judaism including meeting, studying, and worshiping within synagogues. This entire journey God planned before hand to give us even a deeper understanding and appreciation of Judaism as well as the many differences and similarities that have developed since Jesus walked the earth.

I have also worked in the Emergency Services field for over 35 years and retiring at age 51 from the Savannah River Site Fire Department and seeking to follow the LORD full-time where He has for me to minister the rest of my years. As far as education outside of my Fire and EMS training, I have completed an Associate in Science in Criminal Justice in 1983 (University of South Carolina). I completed the Advanced Biblical Studies Diploma from Liberty University in 1990 (Liberty Home Bible Institute), Bachelor of Theology in 1991, a Master of Arts in Biblical Studies in 1996 (American Bible College and Seminary), and a Doctorate in Practical Ministry in Chaplaincy in 2001 (Master's International School of Divinity). I went back to Liberty University and received a Bachelor of Science in Multidisciplinary Studies (Cum Laude) with minors in Criminal Justice and Social Science in 2008. I graduated from the South Carolina Criminal Justice Academy as a Reserve Law Enforcement Officer in 2009. I have Critical Incident Stress Management - Basic, Critical Incident Stress Management - Advanced, & Pastoral Crisis Intervention from the International Critical Incident Stress Foundation. I also completed the Stress and Trauma Care Counseling Certificate Training Program from Light University which is a ministry of the American Association of Christian Counselors. At the time of the writing of this book, I am working on the Graduate Certificate in Judeo-Christian Studies from Master's International School of Divinity.

I believe that God is calling His People back to the walk of the original disciples, back to the Religion of Jesus. This is where the Spirit of God is moving with power as with Jesus and His first disciples. We have to find that same special place. It is a Personal Intimate Relationship and Walk with God the Father by the Power of His Holy Spirit. We need to be in a place where we can hear God clearly and have a Real Personal Powerful Relationship with Him. We need to be in the position to Walk and Do as Jesus did. We, as disciples of Rabbi Jesus, the Messiah, need to become Like Him. God has called me to not only walk like Jesus walked, but to "Help You Reach Your Full Potential In Him".

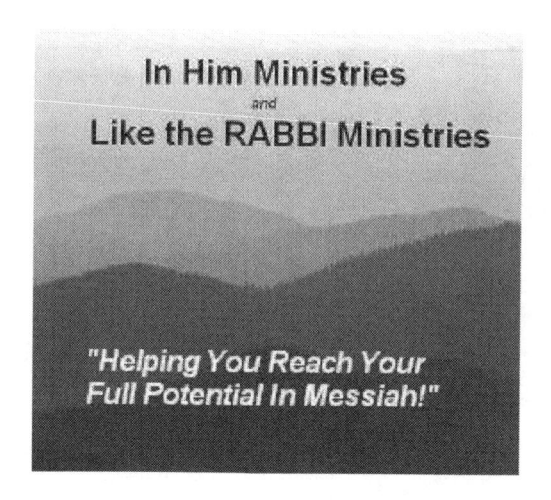

In Him Ministries
and
Like the RABBI Ministries

"Helping You Reach Your Full Potential In Messiah!"

Books by Joseph Chandler:

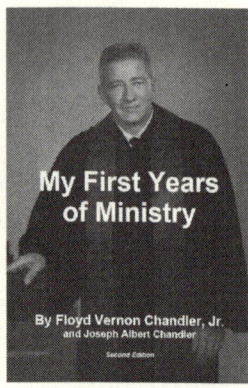

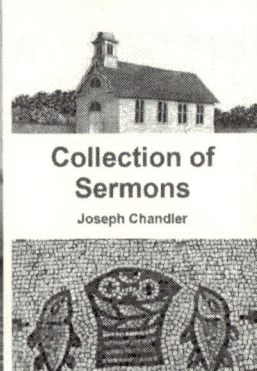

And More Available at:

www.lulu.com

Thanks to My Wonderful Wife
and Partner for Life,
Deidra B. Chandler.

I LOVE YOU!

Joseph Chandler
In Him Ministries
PO Box 449
Jackson, SC 29831
WWW.IN-HIM-MINISTRIES.COM
drjosephchandler@yahoo.com